FOR PEACE AND FOR GOOD

FOR PEACE AND FOR GOOD

A History of the European Province of the Community of St Francis

Helen Stanton

CANTERBURY
PRESS
Norwich

First published in 2017 by the Canterbury Press Norwich
Editorial office
3rd Floor, Invicta House
108–114 Golden Lane
London EC1Y 0TG, UK

Canterbury Press is an imprint of Hymns Ancient & Modern Ltd (a registered charity)

Hymns Ancient & Modern ® is a registered trademark of
Hymns Ancient & Modern Ltd
13A Hellesdon Park Road, Norwich,
Norfolk NR6 5DR, UK

www.canterburypress.co.uk

Scripture quotations are from the New Revised Standard Version of the Bible, Anglicized
Edition, copyright © 1989, 1995 by the Division of Christian Education of the National
Council of the Churches of Christ in the USA. Used by permission. All rights reserved.

British Library Cataloguing in Publication data

A catalogue record for this book is available
from the British Library

978 1 84825 472 5

Typeset by Mary Matthews
Printed and bound in Great Britain by Ashford Colour Press

Contents

Acknowledgements

I would like to express enormous thanks to the Community of St Francis for agreeing that I might undertake this project, and not least for their patience and trust. I would like to thank all those who allowed me to interview them, and also Sisters Helen Julian and Sue for their comments on the manuscript.

Thanks are also due to Christine Smith of Canterbury Press for her considerable patience, and to Mary Matthews and Neil Whyte for their invaluable help with the manuscript.

Thanks to Petà Dunstan for her encouragement and help at the beginning of the project.

I am grateful for the efficient and timely typing of Jo Jackson, and for being able to rely on her confidentiality.

I am also very grateful to The Hosking Houses Trust for awarding me a Writer in Residency, which gave me a place to write and financial support during the earlier stages of the project. Special thanks, too, for the personal encouragement that Sarah Hosking has unstintingly given.

The Queen's Foundation for Ecumenical Theological Education, where I am a tutor, gave me study leave to complete this book. To the Foundation, and its Principal, David Hewlett, I am most grateful, and not least for colleagues like Nicola Slee, Ashley Cocksworth, Eunice Attwood, Andrea Russell, Gary Hall and Debbie Ducille, who have been constantly encouraging. I would also like to give special mention to David Allen, without whom I would have faltered.

The Community of St Clare at Freeland not only gave me a roof over my head when I needed one, but are a true home. Thank you, dear Sisters.

Thanks are also due to many friends: Colin Brady, Beki and Miriam Sellick, Elizabeth Horwell, Natalie Watson, Hannah Cocksworth, Doff

For Peace and for Good

Ward (and for her practical help), Susan Kelley, Rosie Miles, Hannah Ward and Jennifer Wild. Likewise, to members of the community with whom I pray and share my life: the Ewells (Sam, Rosalee, James, Isabella and Katharine), Evie Vernon, Adam North, Andrew Hayes. And finally, enormous thanks to my compañera, Deanna Tyndall, for her continuing encouragement and patience, and (absurdly) to Barak the cat, for pleasant distractions.

Preface

Day 27

The Master says, *'By this everyone will know that you are my disciples, if you have love for one another.'* (John 13.35)

Love is thus the distinguishing feature of all true disciples of Christ. It must be specially an outstanding note in the lives of those who are seeking to be specially consecrated to Christ as his servants. *God is love* (1 John 4.8) and, for those whose lives are *hidden with Christ in God* (Colossians 3.3), love will be the very atmosphere which surrounds all that they do.

(Principles from Day 27)

This is not an exhaustive history: it does not trace minutely the life of every Sister nor every piece of work of the Community of St Francis. It is not communal hagiography. Rather it is a reflection on the life and work of the Community of St Francis, setting that life and work within the context first of the calling and the charism of Saints Clare and Francis, with a nod to Angela of Foligno, and taking both a liberation theology – using the former Franciscan Leonardo Boff – and a Christian feminist reading of these figures. The book also seeks to set the origins of the Community of St Francis within the development of the Catholic revival in the Church of England, which saw the establishment of a distinctively Anglican Religious Life as a token of the authenticity of the Catholicism of Anglicanism. Again a Christian feminist lens is used to examine the extraordinary surge of Anglican women's vocations to Religious Life.

It is with these lenses, which I believe to be particularly appropriate for a Franciscan history, that I retell the story of the origins of the Community of St Francis, and its development under the tutelage and leadership of Rosina Mary, Helen Elizabeth, Agnes Mary and the beginnings of that of Elizabeth. For this phase I am especially indebted to Sister Elizabeth's 1981 history of the Community of St Francis, *Corn of Wheat*, published by Becket Publications, and now out of print. Although Elizabeth takes a very different approach from that of this book, she brings a unique and highly significant voice to this history. Having become a novice in 1956, Elizabeth knew many of the first generations of Sisters, lived with them, and heard them tell of the early years.

Towards the end of Agnes Mary's time as Superior, the Second Vatican Council was called, and revolutionized understandings of Religious Life in the Roman Catholic Church, something that had enormous implications for churches and Religious of other denominations, including Anglicans. My discussion of the changing Life within the Community of St Francis, then, is set within the *aggiornamento* of Vatican II.

As numbers grew, however, and the mission and ministry of the Community of St Francis became more diverse, and more concentrated on small or Branch Houses, its contextual response to God's call became highly complex. For this reason, and also to provide a real flavour of the particularity of these Houses, their work and their concerns, the central chapters of this book focus on two snapshots of the Community, one from 1984 and one from 2004. These chapters offer, lightly edited, extensive excerpts from the House Reports of the time. In these edited verbatim accounts, the voices of various missions and, especially for 2004, of individual Sisters, are heard.

My other major sources for the story of this community are from the archives, mostly extensive but at times fragmentary, and from interviews I conducted. Elizabeth was a key focus for this, but in the end no one voice from the Community predominated, and the analysis and reflection is very much my own.

I interviewed most of the current Sisters, and some former Sisters. I refer to some of this material directly, but do not provide a full account of the interviews. This is because much of the material that emerged was sensitive, sometimes highly sensitive, and so it became more appropriately, I believe, 'deep background' for my reflection, giving it, I hope, a depth and tone that reflect the life of the Sisters.

This is not hagiography, though this process has, I think, given me some glimpses of holiness. Some of it, undoubtedly, is celebratory. Most strongly, however, as I complete this project, I am left with a sense that this Community of female 'Friars' provides significant insight and inspiration into what Christian discipleship might need to look like in the twenty-first century, in order that the whole of God's Church might respond generously and faithfully to the calling of God in the world.

1
Starting Points

Day 1

Jesus the Master speaks, '*Very truly, I tell you, unless a grain of wheat falls into the earth and dies, it remains just a single grain; but if it dies, it bears much fruit. Those who love their life lose it, and those who hate their life in this world will keep it for eternal life. Whoever serves me must follow me, and where I am, there will my servant be also. Whoever serves me, the Father will honour.*' (John 12.24–26)

The Master sets before us in the example of his own sacrifice the secret of fruit-bearing. He surrenders himself to death, and lo! he becomes the source of new life to myriads. Lifted up from the earth in sacrifice, he draws unto him all those multitudes of which the Greeks, whose coming kindled his vision, are the foretaste and prophecy. The life that is cherished perishes: the life that is renounced is eternal. (cf. John 12.20–21)

(Principles Day 1)

To begin at the very beginning would be to start 'primeval-back', with the creation, that revelation of God's goodness to which Genesis 1 and 2 attest; or to begin with the incarnation, God's reconciling of creation with Godself, as God takes our human flesh and thereby restores us to Godself. Both these starting points are significant for Franciscanism: the creation, which Francis saw as fraternal – or by analogy and perhaps better in the context of this book, sororal – in the concept of Brother Sun and Sister Moon; the incarnation too, which Francis experienced so intensely that it marked his flesh with the wounds of Christ, the stigmata, and which is the revelation of God's solidarity with human creation. Francis' personal encounter with Christ focused on the One who was not only 'wounded for our transgressions, crushed for our iniquities' (Isaiah 53.5); but who was the vulnerable child, in the arms of his mother Mary. This child, who, so often, the early Franciscan accounts describe, in corporeal visions that others sometimes witnessed, was entrusted to Francis himself. This experience and devotion may have resulted in the somewhat contentious development of enactments, or *tableaux* of the nativity, an often sentimental aspect of a consumerized Christmas, but the child and the crucified One both represent the limitless costly love of God, to which Francis responded, and called the Church to respond, in a likewise limitless and costly way. The solidarity, or identification, of God with humanity in the incarnation, produced for Francis a response in love for God, whom he encountered 'incarnate' as it were – though he would probably not have used that term – in the poor, those pushed to the margins, not least the lepers of his day. In a manner that might be seen as using the parable of the sheep and the goats (Matthew 25.40ff.) as a paradigm for where the Incarnate One might be encountered, Francis embraced lepers as though they were Christ, and brought into the circle of his understanding the whole of creation, as loved and restored by God through the incarnation. As Sallie McFague was to assert towards the end of the twentieth century: 'Nature is the "new poor"' (McFague, 1993, p. 165).

Beginning with Francis and Clare

That Francis and Clare are essential figures for the Community of St Francis seems obvious, and, as will be seen, they form a vital role in the developing charism of the community. One of the fascinating aspects of my research for this book, however, is that their significance for those who have felt called to the Community of St Francis is very variable. There are those for whom either Francis and or Clare seemed of importance in the early days of their sense of vocation, but more often Sisters have reported to me the significance of meeting Franciscans, men and women; of being inspired by the Community or Society or in some sense having found their home in the Community of St Francis. For some of the Sisters this has resulted in a growing appreciation of Francis and/or Clare, of being inspired by them, even of a palpable sense of being in relation with the founding Father and Mother. For others this appears less significant, and if not seen quite as an accidental or arbitrary coming to Religious Life in a Franciscan form, it is of marginal interest. Being Franciscan women does not necessarily imply a particular interest in Clare, either, and Sisters of the Community of St Francis differ enormously in relation to Clare. For some there is a profound sense of devotion, for some also of respect as a potentially feminist icon. For others, there is a distancing, which may represent a concern to be seen as distinctively First Order, that is Franciscan, Apostolic, or perhaps a wish not to be identified in a feminist framework.

Nonetheless, since the first Rule of the Community of St Francis was adapted – to exclude enclosure – from the Role of St Clare, famously the first Rule for a women's order written by a woman, at least a brief engagement with Clare seems to be required in this book.

Clare and the Community of St Francis

The Community of St Francis, as Apostolic Sisters, that is Religious Sisters who are engaged in apostolic or active ministry, in many ways bears a closer resemblance to a Community of Franciscan Friars than to the first and still extant form of women's Franciscan life, the Poor Ladies, or Poor Clares whose founder, Clare of Assisi, followed Francis. Born in 1194, Clare escaped from the confinement of the life of women among the minor aristocracy and the inevitability of a marriage that would have been intended to enhance her family's wealth and power. Despite the clear piety of Clare's family – or at least the women within it – her encounter with Francis led her to escape into his protection and into what there is some evidence to believe she hoped would be into his way of life. Some believe that Clare was in love with Francis, and certainly as the years passed she demonstrated a clear devotion to him, and he to her. Whatever her motivation in seeking refuge with him, however – and it does bear some resemblance to an elopement story – it was certain that she could not stay with Francis and the small number of Brothers he had gathered around him. The nascent Franciscan community must have seemed eccentric enough, without the scandal of taking in a woman, at a time when unmarried women were regarded as a commodity, whose worth would be sullied by any hint of impropriety.

On 20 March, 1212 Clare escaped through the cellars of her family home, with two female companions, and went to Francis at the Church of the Portiuncula, where Francis received her vows and cut her hair, as a sign that Clare had rejected the life planned for her by her family, and had adopted a Religious Life, not one established and perhaps appropriate to her position in society, but a life unknown.

Sister Frances Teresa, OSC, writes of this moment in the context of the key liberation theology text, the Exodus:

> She [Clare] calls this exodus 'the beginning of my conversion'. She had left a way of life to which she could no longer subscribe, to seek one which expressed the value system she believed to be God's. Liberation theologians have made us much more aware of the sinful drives, greeds and obsessions on which any society is built, and Clare herself had found the values of her social group were no longer tenable, at least by her. She needed to abstract herself from a life based on acquisition and exploitation and to imitate the generosity of God. (Frances Teresa, 1995, p. 18)

Having taken this radical step, Francis and his Brothers immediately took Clare to the Benedictine nuns at San Paolo, near Bastia. This was not only to avoid scandal, but for Clare's protection. Sure enough, the men of her family pursued her to San Paolo where they tried, first by persuasion and then by force, to take her home. The story is told of Clare clinging to the altar – thereby claiming monastic sanctuary – and eventually tearing her veil from her head, revealing her shorn hair, the symbol that she now belonged not to her family, but to God.

Clare's stay at San Paolo was brief but not insignificant, for it indicated not only the seriousness of her intentions, but also that Francis' devotion to poverty had already become a part of her vocation. In the days when Benedictine nuns were divided between Choir Sisters – usually those of high rank and education, who sang the Daily Office and engaged in study as well as prayer, together with a residual element of 'labour' – and Lay Sisters – usually those of lower status and education who focused on the domestic requirements of Religious Life – Clare became a Lay Sister. She not only made this decision, but had ruled out any change of heart or wavering under the requirements of what was often, in effect, tough domestic service, by having given away her wealth, and thereby not having the dowry required to be a Choir Sister.

Clare did not stay long at San Paolo, but, with Francis' help retreated further to the Religious House at Sant' Angelo in Panzo, in the hills above Assisi, where she was joined by her sister, Sister Agnes. The exact nature of this Religious House is disputed, some asserting that it was another Benedictine Community but one that offered Clare more of the solitude she needed, others that it was in fact a *Béguinage* (or *Begijnhof*), one of the less formal, less established, and even experimental houses of religious women, often under temporary vows, which had begun to spring up in the early years of the thirteenth century.

As I have indicated, there is some evidence that Clare had hoped to live a life like that of St Francis and the Brothers. What Francis prepared for her was very different, however, and monastic in the enclosed sense rather than what would today be called an Apostolic Religious Life. Thus it was that after a brief stay at Sant' Angelo, Clare, her Sister Agnes and a few others who had joined them were taken to begin their distinctive Religious Life in a dwelling beside the Church of San Damiano, given for that purpose to Francis by the Benedictines. San Damiano is of considerable significance for Franciscans, women and men, because it was there that Francis received his initial call, to 'Rebuild my church'; and taking his calling literally, Francis restored the fabric of San Damiano with his small group of Brothers. In bringing Clare and her Sisters there, Francis indicated the unity between the two callings, one of the apostolic life of a Friar, the other of the enclosed Poor Ladies, as they were first called, later the Damianites and now the (Poor) Clares. It is not insignificant, therefore, I would suggest, that the Community of St Francis has named its most recent house – in Lincolnshire – San Damiano, a place that brings together the apostolic and the contemplative.

Women's Franciscan life flourished over the centuries, and found apostolic expression in a number of ways. Key in the history of this process were a number of women who belonged to the Third Order of Franciscans, among them Angela of Foligno, who was born in 1248, and after a devastating bereavement developed a life, and a set of followers, who were distinctly apostolic in focus. As Kate Pearson highlights:

> Angela brought her own, woman-shaped, view of personal spirituality and mission, but she also has much in common with the First Order of Franciscans, adopting for all intents and purposes the life of a wandering Friar for herself. Like St Francis, a life of poverty was not an obvious step for her. It seems likely that she was born into a wealthy family and certainly seemed to know much of 'worldly' and sensual pleasures, as evidenced in her writings …
>
> Her conversion experience bears similarities to that of St Francis … [and] as well as the call to poverty, she bears the traditional mark of the Franciscan, is a fascination with the incarnation and a deeply personal and evangelical experience which results in fervent prayer and positive action to serve the poor, teach communities and evangelise. There remains a dedication to a faith that is fully involved and alive in the culture around itself, rather than removed and distant, more focused on finding Christ in the then and now than distinguishing heaven from earth with tight boundaries; this is also Franciscan in its approach, and was a mark of the work of the First Order in their work and ministry as Friars. (Pearson, 2012)

Roman Catholic Congregations

In the early days of the founding of the Community of St Francis, Angela of Foligno did not seem to receive attention, and the recovery of this particular heritage was, therefore, taken up in a much more clearly 'lay' form with the development of the Anglican Third Order in 1936. Alongside Francis and Clare, however, there were two other influences that are important to chart as key to the emergence of the Community of St Francis.

Restoration of Roman Catholic Religious Life in Britain

The first of these was the emancipation of Roman Catholics, beginning at the end of the eighteenth century, when Catholics were no longer regarded as representing a threat to Church and state. From 1778 to 1871, a series of Acts of Parliament relating to both Britain and Ireland allowed for the owning of property and other economic normalization, together with freedom of religious practice devoid of the fines and other sanctions that had been in place. By 1829 Catholics might be elected to Parliament, and by 1871 the repeal of the Test Act enabled Roman Catholic – and incidentally Non-Conformist or Free Church – men to be admitted to British universities.

This more tolerant climate, together with an influx of Irish workers to facilitate the British industrial revolution, brought an increase in the presence of Roman Catholic priests, the re-establishment of monastic foundations, and by the second half of the nineteenth century, the presence of significant numbers of Roman Catholic Apostolic Sisters, whose work often focused on poor Irish communities. Jo Ann Kay McNamara, in her key work *Sisters in Arms: Catholic Nuns Through Two Millennia* (McNamara, 1996), notes the presence of large Apostolic Congregations in England by the final quarter of the nineteenth century, among them the – originally French – Sisters of Charity, the Little Sisters of the Poor and the Faithful Companions of Jesus. In 1846, the Sisters of the Holy Child Jesus was founded in England. These and other Congregations can be found among the inspirers of the development of

Religious Sisterhoods within the Anglicanism of the nineteenth century. McNamara offers a generalized framework for these apostolic orders, similar to the developing Anglican Sisterhoods:

> A congregation usually consisted of a number of small communities growing up in a single locality. A common novitiate in a common mother house formed their charism, that spiritual and vocational character that expressed itself outwardly in tailored devotional practices. A superior general coordinated a rule of life for all houses, which would enshrine their aspirations and guarantee their continuity. (McNamara, 1996, p. 603)

Given the significance, for more recent years of the Community of St Francis, of the ordination of women within the Church of England, of which I shall write more later, it is significant that McNamara sees what she calls 'The embattled [Catholic] Church of the nineteenth and early twentieth centuries ... [as] inclined to enfold nuns into the clerical population while rigorously maintaining their exclusion from the male priesthood' (McNamara, 1996, p. 602). These priestly resonances do not seem to have been made explicit in the development of Anglican Sisterhoods, though it is difficult to imagine they did not exist by the twentieth century, especially with the ordination of Constance Todd Coleman, the first Congregationalist Woman ordained in Britain in 1917, and the appointment, the same year, of the Anglican Maude Royden to be preacher at the City Temple in London.

Deviant Daughters of the Church

Catholic Apostolic Orders may be seen to have been inspirational and influential upon the development of Anglican Religious Sisterhoods generally, but it is specifically within the context of the burgeoning of Anglican Religious Life that the emergence of the Community of St Francis must be seen. Anglican Religious Life emerged almost inevitably from the Oxford Movement and the subsequent liturgical and Anglo-Catholic movements. While Edward Bouverie Pusey was content to 'stand full upon the [Vincentian] canon' for his authority, later Anglicans of a Catholic persuasion felt that the recovery of Religious Life was a legitimizing factor in their assertion of the Catholicity of Anglicanism. Pusey himself wrote:

> It was not *planned* by man: it originated in the providential leadings of God. He began: he carried it on: he gave strength: he will give the increase. It was not the work even of thoughtful persons, judging *a priori* that such institutions would be a blessing to the English Church. It was not planned. It grew ... (quoted in Allchin, 1971, p. 6)

Though I would perhaps add that it was watered, not least by women.

This aspect of providing credentials for Anglo-Catholic developments may well have, more or less consciously, influenced the number of priests who encouraged the founding of Anglican Sisterhoods. As Sister Elizabeth puts it in her MTh dissertation (p. 11): 'Most women's communities in the Church of England had a priest guide or co-founder, who directed their mission and spiritual life and looked after any business transactions.' As will be noted later, this was in part true of the Community of St Francis itself, and it is entirely possible that the founding, or co-founding, of women's Religious Sisterhoods would have been a mark of prestige for a priest in the heyday of Anglican Catholicism.

In fact, the seventeenth-century Anglican divine, Herbert Thorndike, had made the same argument by naming the dissolution of the monasteries 'a blot on the Reformation' (Allchin, 1971, p. 3). Thorndike saw Religious Life as a counter-cultural prophetic 'marker', though in terms of 'a perfection to Christianity' that might not be popular today:

> How great an advantage it is to Christianity to have before the eyes of the world the examples of them that wholly forgo it: to warn them that live in it, to use it as if they use it not; that it is for the service of God, not the satisfaction of themselves. (Allchin, 1971, p. 3)

At the same time, the Anglican Sisterhoods, like the Roman Catholic Congregations, were seen as a vital source of practical ministry, especially among the urban poor. Thus Susan Mumm summarizes Robert Southey's vision for the first of the nineteenth-century Anglican Sisterhoods – the Holy Cross Community:

> he imagined that they would operate as both a refuge and resource: places of refuge for unmarried women and as a source of charitable relief and trained nurses to ameliorate the suffering of the poor. (Mumm, 1999, p. 3)

As Mumm's extensive research – which focuses on the Victorian period and therefore does not include the Community of St Francis – argues, these communities were not simply a refuge for the unmarried daughters of the middle and upper classes, and sometimes the lower classes too, but were also a source of liberation. 'Respectable women', frequently denied the opportunity of work outside the home, were given a recognized and respectable framework in the Sisterhoods, enabling them to work not only with the economically poor, but with other vulnerable groups, like sex workers, itinerants and orphans. Mumm gives an account of life in a Sisterhood that was, for the most part, a liberation from the tedium of middle-class domesticity into a much more exciting world, albeit a world sometimes walled about with regulations that might seem frustrating and incomprehensible. But, as again Mumm makes clear, this access to social work and nursing was often achieved against considerable opposition.

It is difficult, against the background of the late twentieth and early twenty-first century, to imagine quite the level of opposition with which some of the women's Anglican Religious Communities were met. The Anglican Sisterhoods were often associated strongly, and with good reason in many cases, with the liturgical revival that followed the Oxford Movement. This had often been characterized by deeply painful disputes between bishops and what were called 'ritualistic' churches. Ecclesial intransigence on both sides was a characteristic of this time, and there is evidence of bishops refusing to preside at the sacrament of confirmation at such churches, sometimes for years at a time.

There were, of course, exceptions to this, and some sympathetic bishops – it is no accident that Oxford Diocese was home for so many Anglican Religious Communities, both for women and men.

Nonetheless, the reintroduction of not only the centrality of the Eucharist, but a dramatic re-presentation of its 'mystery', using colour, and vestments, processions and even incense in some cases, and focusing on transcendence, was redolent of Roman Catholicism and anathema to much of the heritage of the Enlightenment. Evangelical Anglicanism, likewise frowned upon in some circles for its 'enthusiasm', could still be claimed as an heir of the enlightenment, finding focus in the Bible that might be interpreted in a rational manner, not least by German scholars like David Frederick Strauss, whose *Life of Jesus Critically Examined* was translated into English by George Eliot. By contrast, so-called ritualism came to be associated with a visual flamboyance that was thought scarcely in good taste.

Mumm's work makes clear how horrified some were at the 'corruption' of their daughters by the influence of the growing Catholicism in the Anglican Church, and her book *Stolen Daughters, Virgin Mothers* includes some Victorian cartoons that highlight this horror. A characteristic example of these, from *Punch*, 27 December 1850, pictures predatory priests speaking earnestly to a group of women in a drawing room, one of whom appears to be wearing above her crinoline the veil of a novice. Given the contemporary understanding of women as the weaker and more malleable sex, it is scarcely a wonder that the paterfamilias might fear his daughters, and even his sister, would be contaminated by contact with sex workers and others of dubious provenance. Mumm exposes, too, a sense in the popular mind that Religious Sisterhoods were radically undermining middle-class family life, and women as the angels of the house. In 1847, Alfred, Lord Tennyson's *The Princess* perhaps sums up this spirit in its famous stanza 150:

Man for the field and woman for the hearth:
Man for the sword and for the needle she:
Man with the head and woman with the heart:
Man to command and woman to obey;
All else confusion.

Confusion indeed might prosper if the angel in the house started abandoning the hearth for the street, for social work and nursing, and obeying Mother Church, and even the priestly Father figure, rather than the paterfamilias. Perhaps evangelical daughters caused the same confusion by serving in the missions.

It is easy to caricature the Victorian family, but a horror of Religious Life remains, as tales of many contemporary Religious Sisters and nuns attest. There were not many examples of this among the members of the Community of St Francis whom I interviewed, but there were some. Apostolic Religious Life seems to receive a greater welcome than the enclosed Religious Life, and despite the popularity of such films as *Into Great Silence*, enclosed Religious Life is often met not only with incomprehension but considerable hostility among devout Christians. Perhaps when Elizabeth Stuart sought to expose what she termed collapse of discipleship into family life in an article in 1999, she was mirroring a long-established problem (Stuart, 1999, pp. 9–20), and Religious Life ran counter to this.

Discerning Disciples

Despite the scepticism and hostility with which the first of the Anglican Sisterhoods were often greeted, between the founding of the Sisterhood of the Holy Cross (Park Village) Community – the first of the Sisterhoods – and 1900, Mumm estimates that there had been approximately 90 women's communities – some very short-lived – and approximately 10,000 women who had been members of these communities (Mumm, 1999, p. 3). As I have suggested, the broadening of the life opportunities these Sisterhoods represented was highly significant, and Mumm's work is saturated with accounts of women's enhancement and fulfilment. There was, however, another – and certainly as important – factor that came into play, which was the whole notion of vocation. For the women who joined the Sisterhoods, motivation was clearly varied, some leaving lives that were 'successful', comfortable and fulfilling, others finding in the Sisterhoods a purpose and usefulness, and sometimes an escape from material or emotional poverty. For some of the Sisters whom Mumm cites, talk of God was not highly developed, but practical service was a primary motivation. For others the narratives from the Bible and the tradition, of giving up everything, as Schneiders (2001) puts it, 'Selling All', was enormously significant. Gospel texts such as Matthew 16.24 were inspirational:

> If any want to become my followers, let them deny themselves and take up their cross and follow me. For those who want to save their life will lose it, and those who lose their life for my sake will find it. For what will it profit them if they gain the whole world but forfeit their life? Or what will they give in return for their life?

Matthew 19.29–30 is also found in the correspondence of the day:

> And everyone who has left houses or brothers or sisters or father or mother or children or fields, for my name's sake, will receive a hundredfold, and will inherit eternal life. But many who are first will be last, and the last will be first.

These and other texts were offered in explanation and defence to pious families who viewed the Sisterhoods with incomprehension or worse.

The idea of vocation has been used at various points in the history of the church to empower women, even to protect them when they stepped outside the female norm. Notable among these were medieval women whom we identify as visionaries and mystics. Hildegard of Bingen, for example, a powerful Abbess and preacher, identifies herself as a 'poor weak woman', one who is frail – and she did seem to have poor health – whose visions were, she argued, not of her making but solely from God. This despite the extraordinarily strong words she used to call to account corrupt clergy, and even kings.

Allchin, also emphasizing religious motivation, sees the development of vocations to the Religious Life as the result of:

> the general teaching of the leaders of the Oxford Movement, above all Pusey and Newman, that man (sic) could give himself wholly to

the service and love of God, which led women and men to respond to a call which they heard within themselves to find again the way of dedicated common life in poverty, chastity and obedience. It was this preaching with its urgent call to holiness, coupled with a renewed assurance that the Church of England was part of the One Catholic Church and therefore contained within it unexpected powers of renewal and newness of life, which made it possible for something new, and yet old, to come into existence. (Allchin, 1958)

As has been seen, there may well have been other, more social factors that also contributed to the burgeoning of women's Religious Life, and Sandra Schneiders' summary of what vocation might mean in the context of Religious Life, at least in the late twentieth century, is helpful here. Offering a critique of common understandings of vocation, Schneiders suggests:

When vocation is thought of as a clear call from God indicating what one should do, it carries an implicit threat that failure to obey will have unpleasant if not dire consequences. (Schneiders, 2001, p. 12)

Instead she advances the idea that:

the initiative for considering Religious Life is some kind of 'address', something that calls for a response. But unlike someone suddenly calling my name in a crowded room, the call is coming from both within and from without in a way analogous to the felt call to be an artist or an actor or a scientist. It is a convergence of interior factors such as attraction, talent, experience, desires, ideals, and even realistic fears and awareness of personal limitations, with exterior factors such as people I admire, work that interests me, opportunity presenting itself, needs that move me, structures that facilitate exploration, invitation from another. This convergence is usually a rich mixture that is both confusing and exciting and leads a person to explore what this might mean. (Schneiders, 2001, pp. 12–13)

Into this rich mixture, for significant numbers of those considering the early Sisterhoods, and in part because Anglican Religious Life was so new, came the impetus of religious experience, as something bearing authority, as it had done for the mystics. I am reminded of the exhortation often attributed to Teresa of Ávila, but which is reconfigured by Mirabai Starr, in the 'Introduction' to her translation of the *Interior Castle*:

> This magnificent refuge is inside you. Enter. Shatter the darkness that shrouds the doorway. Step around the poisonous vipers that slither at your feet, attempting to throw you off your course. Be bold. Be humble … Ask no permission from the authorities. Slip away. Close your eyes and follow your breath to the still place that leads to the invisible path that leads you home. (Starr, 2004, pp. 1–2)

Religious experience is by no means the provenance of women only, as the history of early Methodism, for example, attests, but it does seem to provide an extra impetus for those challenging the status quo. Much like the prophet Jeremiah, explaining his unfitness in terms of his youth, it is possible to see nineteenth-century women as ill equipped, by youth or age, by upbringing, for some by lack of experience for the hard physical work often associated with the Sisterhoods, and in some cases with the tough areas and lives they embraced. Although in many ways members, especially the founding members, of the nineteenth-century Sisterhoods were well educated, upper class, used to leadership and arguably quite as well equipped as their fathers and brothers, their motivation often sprang from an intense sense of God's presence and calling. Although not as predominantly atheistic as we are sometimes led to believe, the Enlightenment had left a legacy of the 'high and dry' Church, which was beginning to crumble by the mid nineteenth century and the influence of the Oxford Movement. The evangelical revival and the liturgical movement were both affective movements, which gave more credence to the emotions than had at least the Anglicanism of the eighteenth century. A personal encounter with Christ was a litmus test within evangelical circles, and the focus on the Eucharist in Anglo-Catholic circles embodied that encounter in a tangible, compelling, often aesthetically powerful liturgy. It is fascinating to recognize that this intense and personal religion led so many, from both evangelical and Catholic circles, into a passionate commitment to social reform, expressed in activism, but also a commitment to living with and among the poor. It is to be noted that the heirs of the Enlightenment were not those who made most impact on *Gin Lane*. Whatever the religious extravagances of evangelicals and Catholics, it was the evangelical university settlements, the Salvation Army and the Church Army – as well as the burgeoning Roman Catholic parishes with their apostolic congregations – that were most willing to live and minister among the poor and the 'fallen'.

Written more than a hundred years after the founding of the first Anglican Sisterhoods, Leonardo Boff in his analysis 'For the Poor against Poverty' in *Saint Francis: A Model for Human Liberation*, seems to encapsulate some of the conviction these nineteenth-century disciples lived:

> the option for the poor can be realized in two ways: living with the poor, participating in their struggle for survival, helping them with the profoundly humanizing lenitive of conviviality, even without the perspectives of exterior changes or organizing themselves; and fighting for the cause of their liberation, searching for ways of overcoming poverty toward more just and participatory forms of work and social life. One or the other form expresses love and the desire to take part in the lives of those who have the least, but who are also called to be in communion and fraternity. (Boff, 1982, p. 64)

I will return to Boff's excellent analysis as I explore the specific life of the Community of St Francis.

It might have been possible to view this emphasis on the motivational force of religious experience as a support for the domestication of religion, a 'back to the hearth' movement, to the centre of personal affectivity and devotion. In fact, often it had an opposite effect, expanding a sense of human solidarity and concern, sometimes, as Boff suggests, in challenging the structures of society, as evangelicalism had in an earlier era challenged slavery. There is evidence that a number of founding

Mothers had been interested in and sometimes campaigners for women's suffrage, for example. There was also a strong sense of responsibility for individuals, which emerged from devotion to the God who was made known in Christ, the One who associated with tax gatherers and sinners. As I have mentioned earlier with reference to St Francis, the influence of Matthew 25.40ff. was palpable, of encountering the One who revealed himself among the naked, the hungry, the prisoners. The biblical understanding of the solidarity of Christ with poor people, which Francis had preached, had, in many ways, come into its own.

It is possible to romanticize all this, and the aesthetics of the time certainly contributed to this romanticization. The gothic revival, reclaiming 'Christian architecture' from the 'Pagan' Romanesque style, embodied a return to the medieval, when Christendom flourished. The poetry and painting, which contributed so much to the zeitgeist of the nineteenth century, embraced an earlier age of chivalry, and the quasi-Christian story of King Arthur became of considerable interest. These aesthetic developments did not, it must be admitted, do much to inspire practical Christian mission among women. The drowning Ophelia, the Lady of Shalott, were scarcely role models for nursing Sisters working in a dockland area. The languorous 'beauties' of the Pre-Raphaelite Brotherhood do not suggest a desire to scrub the floors of an orphanage. They do, however, suggest an intensity of response, which, turned away from romantic love, might have inspired the heroic embracing of a challenging life. And there certainly are accounts of women entering Sisterhoods when their aspirations for a lover/husband were thwarted. Though some found the life intolerable, and no substitute for their longings, others found in the Sisterhoods a life where they could flourish and leave regret behind. It was no second best.

Ladies and Sisters

Whatever the motivations – and they will not have been unmixed – of those who joined the Sisterhoods, this was a movement whose time had come. Many of the early Sisterhoods were the projects of the educated upper and upper-middle classes, often of men. This was so of the first of these communities. Founded in 1845, the Sisterhood of the Holy Cross (Park Village) emerged from a committee of the great and the good – all of them men, including Robert Gladstone – but, often seen very much as in response to the work of Robert Southey, who did much to inspire the revival of Religious Life for women in Britain. Mumm sees the failure of Park Village as resulting from what she calls 'foundation by committee'. Yet charismatic women could also be successful as founders, and it is notable that Ascot Priory, which incorporated and superseded Park Village in 1856, was attacked roundly in the press and elsewhere because of its autocratic and aristocratic leader, Lydia Sellon, as well as for its association with 'extreme' ritualistic practices. Despite this ritualist accusation, the Sisters of Ascot Priory in fact responded to a request from the Bishop of Exeter to work in the slums of Devon, and offered a paradigm for future communities. Mumm summarizes their work thus:

> By 1851 Sellon's community, as well as having supplied a number of nurses for Florence Nightingale's hospital in the Crimea, was running an orphanage, a training school for sailor boys, a refuge for girls, a home for elderly seamen, a large industrial school, six model lodging-houses, a soup kitchen, five ragged schools, a convalescent home and a hospital, with sisters working in Devonport, Bristol and Alverstoke in Hampshire. Soon the community was working in Bethnal Green and Bradford on Avon as well. (Mumm, 1999, p. 7)

Bethany

Mumm offers a comprehensive account of Religious Sisterhoods during the Victorian period, among which are the Sisters of Bethany, the Sisterhood at which Rosina, the founder of the Community of St Francis, began her Religious Life. Thus although founded many years before the Community of St Francis, it seems important to touch on some of the key aspects of this Sisterhood.

Founded in 1866, the early Society of the Sisters of Bethany discovered a liturgical focus in embroidery and vestment-making, which was of great significance for the growing liturgical movement within the Church of England. They opened a school of embroidery, and this funded the work of the Sisters in their parish and orphanage. By 1883, the Sisters had begun to work with one of the most influential of the architects and church decorators of the Gothic revival, Ninian Comper. As their website states:

> The Sisters' aim of producing work worthy to stand in the great tradition of English ecclesiastical embroidery was greatly advanced by Comper's guidance and patient training of workers to carry out his exquisite designs.[1]

The results of this partnership are still to be found in Anglican Churches throughout the UK.

As so often during this period, the founder of Society of the Sisters of Bethany, Etheldreda Benett, had in fact begun her Religious Life in another Community, that of the Community of All Saints, Sisters of the Poor, then the largest of the Anglican Sisterhoods. An aristocrat, Etheldreda had considerable qualities of leadership, as a letter quoted in Mumm (p. 58) makes clear. Encouraging Etheldreda to found her own Sisterhood, E. G. Benett (presumably a relative) wrote:

> He [God] has given you a capability of forming a plan beyond many others. Then you have fortune and position in Society as would give you access into the highest ranks ... indeed. You have besides ... a capability of entering into other people's mental distress, which could be all turned to account as the Head of such a Society ... (Mumm, 1999, p. 58)

The emphasis on Etheldreda's own fortune and influence should not be forgotten here, alongside her powers of empathy, and it should be noted that the funding of Anglican Religious Life continues to be a significant issue.

The Society of the Sisters of Bethany was founded in London at Lloyd

---

1 www.sistersofbethany.org.uk/history-of-sisters-of-bethany/vestments-sisters-of- bethany.

Street, Clerkenwell, and it was neither embroidery nor social work that inspired its beginnings, though social work soon became a feature of its life. Rather, to quote again the Sisters of Bethany website:

> Her [Etheldreda's] aim was to 'establish a Community primarily concerned with living the religious life in its integrity, seeking union with God through the knowledge, love and imitation of Our Lord'.[2]

The subsidiary aims were to provide women with opportunities for retreat and to offer regular prayer for the visible reunion of the Church. It was to be a Community of the 'mixed life' of prayer and activity, prayer being the main activity. Pusey and Fr Benson SSJE gave generously of their counsel and encouragement.

Like many of these early Anglican Sisterhoods, Bethany distinguished between Lay and Choir Sisters, as though maintaining a social distinction, but this was not altogether as rigid as might be imagined. A significant number of Lay Sisters at this time were from middle-class families, and took very seriously a calling to a life of poverty, though it is probable that the majority were from poorer backgrounds and might otherwise have been employed as maids. Mumm points to the way Bethany subverted these divisions, so that Lay Sisters served Choir Sisters at table but in turn Choir Sisters served Lay Sisters at table, in order to ensure humility (Mumm, 1999, p. 43). Lay and Choir Sisters were also given equal amounts of time for personal prayer, though almost all of the manual work at Bethany was done by novices and Lay Sisters, and Bethany did all its own work, employing only one person, who fulfilled the role of head laundress (Mumm, 1999, p. 68).

All this provides a context for Franciscan rejection of hierarchical divisions, commitment to living with poor people and identifying with them – a feature of many Sisterhoods – and the development of a 'mixed' community, taking seriously St Francis' Rule for Hermits, together with a commitment to the value of manual or domestic labour.

One other feature of Bethany, which plays rather differently in the development of the Community of St Francis, is the influence of male

---

2 www.sistersofbethany.org.uk/history-of-sisters-of-bethany/ssb-timeline.

clergy and bishops. As I have indicated, the Bethany website emphasizes the influence of the eminent Tractarian, Edward Pusey, and the Founder of the Society of St John the Evangelist (the Cowley Fathers), Richard Benson. However, Mumm insists that one of the distinctive aspects of Bethany's life was its foundation without benefit of the clergy (Mumm, 1999, p. 156–7), and stresses that 'one of Bethany's major contributions was its insistence that women who wished to live the contemplative life within the Anglican Church had the right to do so' (p. 156), perhaps echoing the sentiments of Teresa of Ávila, quoted above. The Community of St Francis was to negotiate this area rather differently, at least at first, as Sister Elizabeth makes clear above, but the autonomy of Anglican women Religious, including later on the Community of St Francis, emphasizes a radical, and perhaps prophetic charism that these women have in common.

Perhaps it is possible to see in these Sisterhoods an eschatological element, as Allchin does of 'Little Gidding':

> a life which is lived always looking towards the end, lived in the spirit of the Gospel parables, being ready for the coming of the Lord like a thief in the night. (Allchin, 1971, p. 5)

The language used in my interviews with members of the Community of St Francis was more that of Evelyn Underhill, however: 'God is always coming to you in the Sacrament of the Present Moment. Meet and receive Him there with gratitude in that sacrament' (Underhill, 1991, p. 186). Certainly for the Sisterhoods, including the as yet unimagined Community of St Francis, it was the ordinary which pointed to the transcendent, and properly for a Christian Community whose charism was in the way of St Francis, it was among those of no account Christ could be met and embraced.

2
Beginnings and Endings

Day 10

The Master, who, coming into the world not to do his own will but the will of him that sent him, *became obedient to the point of death – even death on a cross* (Philippians 2.8), says to those who follow him,

'Take my yoke upon you, and learn from me; for I am gentle and humble in heart, and you will find rest for your souls.' (Matthew 11.29)

The Brothers and Sisters desire, therefore, to surrender their wills to the will of God, in the spirit of perfect obedience, that being delivered from self-will and pride they may find true freedom and peace and be ready instruments which he can use for his purposes.

(Principles Day 10)

If the roots of the Community of St Francis began in one sense at creation and the incarnation, and in another with the lives of Francis and Clare, and in the context of the revival of Religious Life in England, it also, and perhaps more obviously, makes sense to trace that life back to the time when at the Society of the Sisters of Bethany, the 21-year-old Rosina Rice was professed as a Lay Sister, on 17 October 1884. Rosina joined the new Bethany convent, built in 1881, at Clerkenwell, where the Sisters simultaneously worked, as has been described, among the poor, encouraging the retreat movement and serving the liturgical movement through their embroidery work. As significantly for *this* story, some of the Sisters began to work in the parish of the Holy Redeemer, Clerkenwell. Built in 1888, and designed by John Dando Seddon, its website states:

The church was built like so many other Anglo-Catholic missions according to the ideals of the Oxford Movement, and like some of its Gothic Revival counterparts was intended to rise up cliff-like and remind the whole neighbourhood of its presence. One is reminded particularly of St Columba Haggerston and St Peter Vauxhall, two other outstanding buildings in poor neighbourhoods like Clerkenwell was at that time. The church felt that the poorest neighbourhoods should get the best churches.

Interestingly it was at St Peter's Vauxhall, from 1865, that the first Sisters of the Community of the Holy Name worked; another example, perhaps, of how the poorest neighbourhoods seemed to attract Religious Sisters as well as notable architects.

The Sisters of Bethany provided a place that nurtured Sister Rosina's vocation, and in which she found her call developed and sustained for many years.

It was at least in part because of her commitment to poverty and humility that Sister Rosina chose to became a Lay Sister, since, as Sister Elizabeth attests (Elizabeth CSF, 1981, p. 8), her later writing for the Community of St Francis novitiate was far from unscholarly. There is also, I believe, a resonance here with the story of St Clare, who, as I have described above, when taken to the Benedictines at San Paulo became a Lay Sister, having already given away her fortune in order, perhaps to resist the temptations of a more comfortable – at least materially – life of a Choir Sister, something more common for one of her social status. There is no evidence of Sister Rosina's awareness of St Clare's story, but perhaps it might be possible to recognize something serendipitous here.

At the Sisters of Bethany, too, Sister Rosina met the woman who was to help focus a different calling and in many ways inspired Rosina to leave Bethany to found the Community of St Francis. Lurana Mary White had tried her vocation in two communities in her native United States of America, first at the Community of the Sisters of the Holy Child, in Albany, and then at the Community of St Mary at Peekskill. In due course, she came to England with an aunt and asked to try her vocation with the Sisters of Bethany. Mother Etheldreda, Superior at the time, and a woman both formidable and wise, gave Lurana permission to become a postulant, on the understanding that she would in all probability return to the United States to found a different Anglican community. At this time aspirants to the Religious Life were often postulants for a very brief time, but Lurana remained in this state for several months before her return to the United States, where, with appropriate guidance, she was involved in the beginnings the Society of the Atonement, a Sisterhood, and indeed Brotherhood, with a strong Franciscan flavour.

For both Sister Rosina and Lurana a Franciscan charism began to grow, encouraged by the influence of Cyril John Hawes, an architect, who in turn was influenced by James Adderley – founder of the Society of the Divine Compassion, which was to develop into the Society of St Francis.

Hawes was persuaded in 1901 to train to be an Anglican priest, and after considering becoming a Benedictine, under the tutelage of Aelred Carlyle, he was sent by the Bishop of Northumberland as curate at Holy Redeemer Clerkenwell.

Like Sister Rosina and Lurana, Hawes had a strong sense of solidarity with poor people and rather eccentrically chose to live not in the simplicity of the parish clergy house, but rented a small and by all accounts somewhat unwholesome room in a lodging house, refusing to accept his full stipend and giving away most of his possessions. During this period Hawes, Sister Rosina and Lurana became friends, and the attraction to a life of poverty was given greater impetus. When Lurana returned to the United States, she and Sister Rosina were to correspond regularly and to influence one another's thinking.

In 1905 Sister Rosina applied to her Superior in the Sisters of Bethany and with her permission sought to live a life of greater austerity away from the convent at Lloyd Square. Sister Rosina was accompanied by a fellow, but far more junior, Lay Sister, Sister Hannah, and two other women, about whom little is known before their association with Sister Rosina's group. Again there are parallels with Clare, for this little group at first lodged with Benedictines, in their case the Sisters of the Holy Comforter at Edmonton, who later moved to West Malling.

The generosity and friendliness with which Sisterhoods seem to have regarded those who left to found other Communities is somewhat surprising, but perhaps reflects the history of these movements, where vows, especially life vows, were initially viewed with suspicion, and obedience in particular was often regarded as 'papist' and therefore dubious. There was, at least among those who remained Anglican, little sense of alarm let alone of betrayal or bad blood between those who remained and those who left. In the case of Sisters Rosina and Hannah and their companions, there was of course initially no sense of a 'split' nor of a rebellion or rejection of the Society of the Sisters of Bethany, rather their sense of a compelling vocation to greater poverty and solidarity with poor people seems to have been convincing. By this stage too Sister Rosina was highly experienced, professed some 18 years, who though lay, as has been described, had lead a Religious Life closely related to that of Bethany's Choir Sisters.

Thus it was that on 20 February 1905, Sisters Rosina and Hannah went to see the Bishop of London, the Rt Revd Winnington Ingram, and the Community of St Francis received its imprimatur. The date associated with the foundation is 25 February 1905, though there is no unassailable evidence of this precise dare. The nascent community adopted the brown habit of the Franciscans and adopted the Rule of St Clare, with the exception of enclosure, as Apostolic Sisters, effectively becoming friars, though the adoption of St Clare's not St Francis' Rule suggests that the claim of Sisterly Brotherhood was not in their minds, or may have been a claim too far. It should be noted here that the Community of St Francis never adopted the Rule of St Francis, although the original Rule did include some parts of it.

The Rule

St Clare's Rule seems remarkably short in comparison with, say, that of St Benedict, but it is of enormous historic significance, not least for the history of women's Religious Life, in that St Clare is generally believed to have been the first woman to write a Rule for a women's Order. Initially Clare's point of reference was, not surprisingly, St Francis, and in her own Rule she apparently quotes him, offering his and the Brothers' commitment to the Ladies, as part of what might be called the Franciscan 'family':

> Since by Divine authorisation you have made yourselves daughters and servants of the most high King, the heavenly Father, and have taken the Holy Spirit as your spouse, choosing to live according to the perfection of the holy Gospel, I resolve and promise for myself and for my Brothers always to have that same loving care and special solicitude for you as [I have] for them. (Armstrong, 1982, p. 218)

Mother Rosina Mary, foundress.

The closeness of relationships between the early Franciscan Brothers and the Poor Ladies was mutually significant, and though for the reasons at which I have already hinted the women were enclosed, the Brothers regularly visited the Sisters and occasionally St Clare at least was able to visit St Francis, something that became very precious to both of them, especially towards the end of Francis' life. The Brothers not only acted as spiritual advisers to the Sisters but were also recipients of alms and prayerful support. The Brothers and Sisters in medieval times had to fight hard for this level of intimacy, since impropriety was imagined everywhere. As becomes clear in the history of the Community of St Francis, this suspicion was overcome, and Brothers and Sisters of St Francis came to relate to each other and indeed sometimes to share houses and ministries together, rather later in their respective histories. When these developments took place, it was also clear that there was a far greater sense of mutuality and equality than these words of Francis above suggest.[3]

Later on in Chapter 6 of St Clare's Rule, more words of St Francis are quoted, this time on the more obvious but highly significant issue of poverty, which I will discuss further in the next chapter:

> I, Brother Francis, the little one, wish to follow the life and poverty of our most high Lord Jesus Christ and of His most holy mother and to persevere in this unto the end; and I ask and counsel you, my ladies, to live always in this most holy life and in poverty. And keep most careful watch that you never depart from this by reason of the advice or teaching of anyone. (Armstrong, 1982, p. 218)

This focus on poverty was St Clare's key requirement, and because of it, she spent much energy in challenging the Catholic authorities for what she called 'the privilege of poverty'. There remained throughout her life real pressure from church authorities for the convents established under the influence of Saints Clare and Francis to collect tithes from tenants and

---

3 The SSF Brothers played a far greater role in the foundation of the Community of St Clare, the enclosed Clare community now at Freeland in Oxfordshire, though there too, any paternalistic tendencies met with a robust response from strong women who knew their own minds.

farms. While mendicant Friars might just be acceptable to the respectable world of the Church, mendicant women were not, and as I have already suggested, the Church felt the need to guarantee a respectable and appropriate life for women often from the upper classes and aristocracy – St Clare's most famous protégée was Agnes of Prague, also known as St Agnes of Bohemia, daughter of the King of Bohemia. In her book *The Privilege of Poverty* Joan Mueller makes clear that:

> The papacy ... wanted the Sisters to have greater ecclesiastical stability and dignity. To this end, both Gregory IX and Innocent IV endowed Damianite monasteries with property holdings. Most Damianites willingly accepted these land grants with the accompanying style of life. (Mueller, 2008, p. 105)

St Clare, however, had been adamant in rejecting such an idea, as had Agnes, but many of their Protectors after the death of St Francis tried to make them conform to a Rule that looked very much like that of St Benedict, and avoided the question of poverty. Pope Gregory IX felt that St Clare's intransigence in this regard might have been caused by her vow, made to Francis, of absolute poverty. He therefore offered to absolve her from this vow of absolute poverty and she famously replied, 'Holy Father, I crave for absolution from my sins, but I desire not to be absolved from the obligation of following Jesus Christ.'

It is uncertain whether St Clare was granted this most passionate of her requests, but it is generally accepted that after the death of Pope Gregory, she was forced to request this 'privilege' again from the next Pope, Innocent. Two days before her death Innocent finally confirmed the Rule of the Clares (Bull, 'Solet Annuere', 9 August, 1253), granting her and her Sisters the absolute poverty she saw as key to the vocation of the Damianites.

Obedience

Alongside the vow of poverty, Clares, and in turn the Sisters of the Community of St Francis, like all but Benedictines, vowed themselves to celibacy and obedience. I will discuss celibacy alongside prayer at some length in Chapter 9. The modern focus on obedience as 'community listening' seems not to have been part of everyone's story of the early days of the Community of St Francis. Virginia Nicholson's account of Rosamund Essex's time with the Community of St Francis offers a highly unsympathetic reading of the Community as Essex experienced it, though it must be noted that Nicholson's view of Christianity generally is somewhat jaundiced. Writing of a difference of opinion with Reverend Mother Elizabeth, Rosamund Essex notes:

> And, she [Revd Mother] went on to: 'You must not only say what I say, *but you must believe that it is right.*' I could not think a thing true which was not. I said so. I was very soon dismissed from the community. And a good thing too. I was far too individualistic, far too independent, far too disinclined to blind obedience to fit into the Religious Life. (Nicholson, 2008, p. 248; original emphasis)

This is a very different testimony from that of Sister Elizabeth, who asserted that there was little difference between monastic obedience and the obedience required at home. Again Nicholson states:

> Whatever it was that caused her [Rosamund Essex] to offer herself as a postulant nun to a small Franciscan Order in Dalston, it was a disaster from the start. 'Never', writes Essex, 'could there have been so unsuitable … a candidate.' The tyranny, harassment and pettiness of convent life caused her to boil with rage; the lack of common sympathy and kindness baffled her and shook her convictions. Austerity – cold, hunger, discomfort, hard work and exhaustion – she could cope with, but inhumanity, verbal abuse, intellectual starvation, pettiness and unreasoning obedience were asking too much. (pp. 247–8)

The issue of intellectual starvation recurs in a number of the tales of those who have left the Community of Saint Francis, as does the issue of infantilization, though there have remained many who have published and who speak of finding contentment in the Community after prolonged careers as, for example, senior grammar school teachers. And intelligence is valued, one Sister insisting that brains are to be used, not neglected in the Religious Life. Certainly it is true that St Francis valued the poverty of Christ and identification with poor people who were the face of Christ above all else, and he forbade his Brothers to have a library. This apparent anti-intellectualism disappeared fairly early on in the medieval history of Franciscans, however, and some of the foremost of mediaeval theologians and philosophers, like Bonaventure and Duns Scotus, were Franciscan.

Nonetheless, it is significant that St Clare states that the illiterate should not seek to acquire literacy, but rather recite by heart the prayers they knew and regard that as enough to join with the following of the way of Jesus and Francis.

'And those who do not know how to read should not be eager to learn. Rather let them devote themselves to what they must desire to have above all else: the Spirit of the Lord and His holy manner of working, to pray always to Him with a pure heart, and to have humility, patience in difficulty and weakness, and to love those who persecute, blame, and accuse us; for the Lord says: *Blessed are they who suffer persecution for justice's sake, for theirs is the kingdom of heaven* (Matthew 5.10). *But he who shall have persevered to the end will be saved* (Matthew 10.22)' (Armstrong, 1982, pp. 222–3).

It should be noted that in Anglican women's communities scholarship tends to be most treasured among those who are enclosed or regarded as contemplative, but this does not necessarily preclude Apostolic Sisters.

Although in an unguarded moment Sister Elizabeth has talked of other – than Rosamund Essex's – disastrous novitiates, and novices, there is also a strong sense among those who have remained that – and sometimes despite degrees of pettiness and personal unkindness – Religious Life, and that which finds its expression within the Community of St Francis, also provides a framework for flourishing and expansiveness as well as of containment. I am reminded of Alison Phipps' comment relating to her Rule of Life as a member of the Iona community: 'It is not that I keep the Rule. It is that the Rule keeps me.'

Practicalities

St Clare's Rule is both compassionate and specific. It states that the

Poor Ladies are to make their confession 12 times a year, and receive communion seven times, both of which sound arcane to twenty-first-century ears, though the gift of the sacrament of reconciliation is practised among some of the Sisters today, and communion is received very regularly by both lay and ordained Sisters. Indeed the Catholic Anglican practice of daily communion is practised by some. One of CSF's priest Sisters was once heard agreeing with a member of the Presbyterian Church that the Eucharist was to be taken so seriously that communion should be received either daily or very rarely indeed.

Of course, in the medieval Church there was a practice of attending Mass regularly but receiving communion sparingly, in part because of a sense of unworthiness.

Regulations are made for the election of an Abbess, and for those who were what today might be called extern Sisters. In a sense all Sisters of the Community of St Francis were and are extern Sisters, in that they are not enclosed, and so injunctions like the wearing of shoes come into play, though some Sisters do go barefoot into chapel, and among some Sisters the habit of wearing sandals not shoes still applies.

I am struck by the good sense of some of the injunctions of St Clare's Rule, for example not having favourites, the failure to avoid which has been problematic at times in the Community of St Francis.

Overall, however, there is a sense of flexibility in the Rule, which is surprising and contrasts markedly with Nicholson's account of Rosamund Essex's experience. Throughout the Rule there are examples of practices that are modified by the word 'except' and refer to Sisters who are particularly under pressure or enduring ill health. There is a strong sense of the Abbess as the mother figure, who will interpret the Rule as is appropriate for individuals.

> Regarding the sisters who are ill, the Abbess is strictly bound to inquire with all solicitude by herself and through other sisters what [these sick sisters] may need by way of counsel and of food and other necessities and, according to the resources of the place, she is to provide for them charitably and kindly. 8. [This is to be done] because all are obliged to serve and provide for their sisters who are ill just as

they would wish to be served themselves if they were suffering from any infirmity. 9. Each one should make known her needs to the other with confidence. For if a mother loves and nourishes her daughter according to the flesh, how much more lovingly must a Sister love and nourish her Sister according to the Spirit! (Armstrong, 1982, p. 220)

Now of course, the golden rule might leave much to be desired if some Sisters are much more robust than others, but the emphasis here on compassion is striking. St Clare's chapter on the strongly titled Chapter X, 'The Admonition and Correction of the Sisters', puts this compassionate approach into even more focused light:

On her part, the Abbess is to be so familiar with them [the Sisters] that they can speak and act toward her as ladies do with their servant. For that is the way it should be, that the Abbess be the servant of all the sisters. (Armstrong, 1982, p. 222)

Developments

However well or badly this pattern of leadership was managed the Community of St Francis Rule evolved over the years. From the beginning, the community leader was Revd Mother rather than Abbess, as was the case in the other Sisterhoods of the nineteenth and early twentieth centuries – the term Abbess after all referring to a monastic community not to an Apostolic Sisterhood. Following the terminology that emerged from Vatican II, and which influenced the world of Religious Life, Catholic, Anglican and Protestant, Sister – then Mother – Elizabeth, following the Brothers of the Society of St Francis, instituted the concept of the Guardianship of Houses, instead of the title Sister in Charge, and of Provinces – Elizabeth becoming Minister Provincial and styling herself Sister.

The evolving Rule of Life evolved also as the Sisters gained a greater sense of relationship with other Franciscan groups, and the Community of St Francis' growing relationship with Franciscan Brothers began in 1942 when Brother Algernon (Algy) of the Society of St Francis became Warden. The Community of St Francis continued to be a much smaller grouping than the SSF, and might have easily been swamped, but strong and independently minded leadership, and Sisters more generally, together with a certain awareness of power dynamics among the Brothers, meant that it was for the Sisters to request a closer and formal relationship with the Brothers. Petà Dunstan, in *This Poor Sort: A History of the European Province of the Society of St Francis*, records, 'From 1963, the Sisters were mentioned in the first paragraph of the SSF Manual and considered "part of the SSF family"', though the link was not formalized and Dunstan describes the Society of St Francis chapter as regarding 'the Sisters as "under the care of the Brothers"' (Dunstan, 1997, p. 232). The Sisters might not have used these precise terms. When in May 1970 it was suggested that the Community of St Francis become First Order Sisters of the Society of St Francis, the Sisters responded with some interest but were determined to preserve their autonomy and distinctiveness. It is notable that they chose to retain the title Community of St Francis, in part to maintain this distinction, despite recognizing themselves as part of the Society, alongside the Brothers, the Community of St Clare – in some ways an even more distinctive group – and the flourishing Third Order.

Nonetheless it is notable that the Community of St Francis' first religious and priestly advisor was the Benedictine Aelred Carlyle, whom Petà Dunstan describe as 'flamboyant ... charming and charismatic' (Dunstan, 2009, p. 1), rather than a Franciscan Brother, and although Cyril John Hawes knew and admired James Adderley of the Society of the Divine Compassion, there was no contact until much later between the women and men of the Anglican Franciscans. It may well be, too, that both Hawes and Carlyle were more familiar with Benedictine nuns and Sisterhoods influenced by the Benedictine Rule, and so something at least deriving from the world of women's enclosure seemed more appropriate to them. Nonetheless, like St Clare before them, the Community of St Clare rejected this and also resolutely refused the ownership of property.

Nonetheless, Carlyle's conversion to the Rome Catholic Church in 1909, with most of his Benedictine Brothers at Caldey Island, five years after the Community of St Francis gained official recognition, was to be significant for the Sisters. But in late 1905, Carlyle's intervention in their lives was significant still within an Anglican framework when he facilitated an invitation from the Revd Arthur English to work among poor people in the parish of Sculcoates in Hull.

If the embracing of poverty was misunderstood in the early modern times in which Francis lived, it was also suspected towards the end of the nineteenth and beginning of the twentieth century, when at least one of the objections to the apostolic Religious Life for women was that respectable middle-class women would be exposed to the physical and 'moral' contamination that life in the slums, it was thought, would inevitably bring. It was in such an environment that the Community of St Francis went to live in the parish of Sculcoates.

Sister Elizabeth describes the development thus:

> It was an ideal situation to which the tiny group moved, late in 1905 or early 1906; a dockland parish where they soon won the hearts of the families around them. St Mary's is a Victorian church and has a chapel dedicated to St Francis. The Sisters lived at number 77, Nicholson Street, quite close to the river, a dingy area of reclaimed marshland, with narrow streets and railway sidings. Here they took in laundry to pay their rent, adapting a shed down the backyard for a laundry. They also visited the sick and looked after children while their mothers were working or attending Church and Mothers' Union meetings ... The Community called their convent St Damien's, in memory of the first convent of Franciscan Sisters in Assisi, and though perhaps the name was the only resemblance, no doubt the idea brought encouragement to those who lived there.
>
> They considered themselves very much the daughters of St Clare ... (Elizabeth CSF, 1981, p. 12)

Sister Elizabeth, quoting Sister Margaret Mary, sees these early few years as being especially inspired by the medieval founders, and again takes up the theme of poverty:

> The life started by St Clare and her companions was one in which poverty and simplicity were the decisive factors ... Absolute poverty, trust in God and a readiness to do any work, however simple, which

34

came her [Clare's] way, were the principles of her life up to the very end. It was not only in the true ideal of the cloistered life that her power was felt; women, and men too, in all ranks, recognised the beauty and simplicity which radiated from St Damian's and longed to follow. (p. 12)

Despite the hardships, there were those who followed the Sisters to Hull, among them Helen Christmas, who was to become Sister Helen Elizabeth in Religious Life, and who became a novice in 1907 and brought the skills and experience of professional nursing – at Guy's Hospital in London – to the Community, as well as playing a highly significant part in the Community's survival.

The Sisters were in Sculcoates for a very brief period, and there is some mystery regarding their decision to leave Hull for Dalston, London, in 1907. Sister Elizabeth, in emphasizing the importance of episcopal support, perhaps suggests that this was not much in evidence in Hull. It is certainly true, as will be seen in relation to the Sisters of the Incarnation in Birmingham, that some bishops were far from happy with the development of Religious Life in the Church of England. Franciscans still find themselves fundamentally independent of ordinary church structures, though they seek to build good relationships with local structures, bishops and parish clergy. In the early 1900s, this was essential. As Sister Elizabeth states:

Their [Carlyle and Hawes'] own experiences in trying to establish the religious life as they envisioned it had made them realise the importance of proper recognition. Most sensibly they impressed the Sisters at St Damian's with the absolute necessity of obtaining episcopal approval and sanction. Without it, the Community could have no stability or permanent status. (p. 14)

Despite their technical independence, the Sisters of the Community of St Francis' history attests that their presence and assistance have been much in demand among parish clergy and bishops, often though not always to work among the poorest. In fact far more invitations have been received than it has been possible to meet. Like many Religious they continue to celebrate their independence, and have sometimes been able to take on projects that might be seen as risky among those for whom the status of the Church is of greater importance.

Recreation at Dalston.

In the early years of the twentieth century, the recognition of Religious Communities to ensure their growth and establishment seems at least to have influenced the move of the Community of St Francis back to London, and to their long-standing home in the parish of St Philip's, Dalston. Again the move was influenced by Dom Aelred Carlyle, and the Sister's long-standing mentor, Cyril John Hawes, now Brother Jerome. Reservations about Mother Rosina Mary and her Sisters in relation to Dalston were set out in a letter from Charles Thornely, Anglican parish priest of St Philip's, Dalston, dated 11 November 1907, suggesting perhaps that the Bishop of Stepney was also not too keen on unknown Religious moving into the diocese.

Dear Madam,

I think you already know that Dom Aelred has suggested my asking you to come and work in this parish. I have been earnestly thinking over the matter and making some enquiries, also trying to find a way of ensuring sufficient funds.

The Bishop of Stepney writes: 'He is not very anxious on principle to encourage a small Sisterhood unconnected with the Diocese to come to London. But before saying more he would be glad to know why they are leaving their present work.'

In reply I sent him Mr England's letter to me which will explain your position. I shall be glad to hear anything from you which I may put before him. I understand that the Bishop of London is acquainted with your work.

I am also doubtful until I hear from you, whether this parish is exactly what you would find best for yourselves. It consists of a large number of lower middle class and poor, almost equally divided. The population is between 11,000 and 12,000, and there is much good work to be done.

The presence of Sisters is, of course, an untried experiment in this parish, but there is no reason why it should not prove a great blessing. One has to feel one's way with our class of people.

I do not know what you are accustomed to in your church at Sculcoates. We have, of course, daily Mass, and Sung Mass every Sunday; of externals we have not much, bit I try to insist on careful and persistent teaching of the Faith, while the Church itself is kept as the centre of our life, and we build upon visiting and teaching. I do not therefore promote organisitions, if I can avoid them.

I should be so very glad to meet you and discuss the whole question with you. Are you likely to be in or near London before long?

Yours faithfully in our Lord

(Signed) Charles E. Thornely (Elizabeth CSF, 1981, p. 15)

It is possible to see this letter as cautious, or as equivocal. It did, however, set in motion conversations and correspondence between the Bishops of Stepney and London and Rosina, who travelled to London to visit Charles Thornely. With the recommendation of the Bishop of London, and after examination of the Rule of Life and Office Book, permissions were granted. To quote Sister Elizabeth: 'they all prayed and discussed the whole matter before a decision was made to move to Dalston' (Elizabeth CSF, 1981, p. 15). There is no sense here of autocratic decisions made between the men and Mother Rosina Mary – again, perhaps, evidence of an early independence.

Meanwhile Charles Thornely's response to the project became much more enthusiastic. Again to quote Sister Elizabeth:

> He [Thornely] rented a small house on a year's lease, 65 Malvern Rd, some rooms of which he had stripped and whitewashed as the Sisters wanted, but he wrote that they would have to put up with some 'cheerful' wallpapers left in other rooms. He applied to the East London Church Fund for a grant of £20 per annum for a parish worker but said he would invite them regardless. 'Without it', he said, he would only 'have to beg the harder.' He had one room prepared as an oratory and the floor stained, but would not have gas fittings ended until the Sisters moved in, as it was not advisable to leave such in an empty house. (p. 15)

Slightly delayed by a commitment in Hull, Sister Helen Elizabeth arrived in Dalston on 9 March 1908, followed by the others. Ten months later, the Bishop of London, Cosmo Lang, received the life professions of Sisters Helen Elizabeth and Elizabeth Clara, and the small group felt themselves established.

Sisters of the Community? The Sisters of the Incarnation of the Eternal Son

The Community of St Francis was not the only Sisterhood with a Franciscan charism. While Lurana and Sister Rosina were working together with their Sisters in solidarity with poor people in Clerkenwell, another group of putative Franciscan women were gathering together, influenced also by James Adderley. Adderley had left Oxford to pursue a career in law, but had become increasingly attached to the work of the Church in the East End of London, in the Oxford University Mission based at Oxford House, Bethnal Green. In 1887, Adderley went to be curate at St John's, Bethnal Green, where he met the sister of the St John's vicar, Gertrude Brombey.

When Adderley became vicar of St Philip's, Plaistow, Gertrude moved to live in that parish and, as Barrie Williams puts it, 'Here she began a remarkable ministry of compassion, visiting the poor, nursing the sick and running a club for boys' (Williams, 1982, p. 63). In 1898, Gertrude was professed as Mother of a small community that had developed and was dedicated as the Sisters of the Incarnation of the Eternal Son.

The Sisters followed Adderley on his various moves both in London and later to Birmingham, where they worked in Adderley's parishes as well as developing other ministries, notably, in Birmingham, an orphanage, something for which Mother Gertrude had to struggle for support from what Williams calls '[t]he civic authorities' (p. 65). Eventually she, too, had to struggle to find the support of the Church, as had, perhaps, Rosina Mary in Hull. The first Anglican Bishop of Birmingham, Charles Gore, was like many of those I write of in this book, not least the nascent Franciscans: both Anglo-Catholic and committed to social reform. His support for Gertrude and her Sisters was, therefore, enthusiastic, and in fact he encouraged them to move to Birmingham. On this occasion Hawes joined the Sisters and not vice versa. This support continued under Russell Wakefield who was Anglican Bishop of Birmingham in 1911–24. His successor, however, Ernest Barnes, took a different view of Catholic tendencies in the Church of England, and of the Religious Life more specifically. Initially a mathematician, Barnes was a theological liberal and his resignation was called for, but not accomplished, when he not only questioned the Virgin birth but also the bodily resurrection of Jesus. Ernest Barnes was also sceptical about the Real Presence in the Eucharist, and Anglo-Catholic practices such as the Reservation of the Blessed Sacrament, which he tried to eradicate from the Anglican Diocese of Birmingham. The implications of this for the Sisters of the Incarnation of the Eternal Son meant, as Williams puts it: 'Barnes ... forbade the Sisters to have any "rebel" priest to celebrate the Eucharist for them – and many Catholic-minded priests in his diocese were driven to become rebels. Worse, he refused to receive the profession of any Sister, and numbers consequently declined. Dr Barnes later modified his attitude, but the damage was already done' (Williams, 1982, p. 65). The community met with many adversities during Barnes' prelature, not least being hit by a bomb in 1940, and in 1964 the remaining Sisters moved to the Community of the Holy Name, by then in Malvern.

What is fascinating for the purposes of this book is that there was so little contact between the Society of the Incarnation of the Eternal Son and the Community of St Francis, and that in its decline the Sisters of the Incarnation of the Eternal Son turned to the 'mixed' but significantly Benedictine-influenced Community of the Holy Name rather than the Community of St Francis.

Conversion

Throughout this period, and perhaps one of the reasons for the scepticism of some Anglican bishops, there was a strong movement within the Catholic wing of the Church of England that longed for union with the Roman Catholic Church, and saw this as the final vindication of the Catholic nature of the Anglican Church. Individuals, parishes and Religious Communities and Orders saw the strengthening of Religious Life within the Church of England as an earnest that this longing would be fulfilled. This movement, in a form often called 'Anglo-Papalism', though the term sounds somewhat derogatory, hoped and worked for a unity with Roman Catholicism that might be achieved by a wholesale 'return' of Anglicanism to the Mother Church of Rome, rather than a piecemeal conversion individual by individual or parish by parish.

Petà Dunstan, in her book about the Benedictines of Pershore, Nashdom and Elmore (Dunstan, 2009), tells the story of how again and again Anglicans of a Catholic persuasion were discouraged in this vision, and, unable to hold on until the day when Anglicans en masse might take their full place in the Roman Catholic Church, began to move directly into that Church. This process had, of course, happened from almost the beginning of the Oxford Movement, when probably Anglo-Catholicism's most famous convert, the Blessed John Henry, Cardinal Newman, found his position as a Catholic Anglican untenable. At times during the end of the nineteenth and beginning of the twentieth centuries this trickle of coverts became a steady stream, and by 1909 Mother Rosina Mary and some of her Sisters, like many others, became convinced that they could not remain within the Anglican Church.

Like the founding of the Community of St Francis in the first place, Mother Rosina's call to another configuration of Religious Life was clearly influenced by her relationship with Lurana White. By this time the (Franciscan) Society of the Atonement, in the United States of America, and of which Lurana was Reverend Mother, was promoting church unity in the spirit of the 'Anglo-Papalists' in the hope that the Anglican Church would seek conversion to the Roman Catholic Church. Also, Sister Elizabeth records that Mother Rosina was troubled by St Francis' vow, in his Primitive Rule, of loyalty to Pope Innocent III and his successors, and wondered whether in order to be truly Franciscan her small community should live in accordance with that vow. Clearly at the heart of this was a profound questioning of the Catholicity of the Anglican Church. When Mother Lurana in 1909, together with the entire community of Brothers and Sisters of the Society of the Atonement at Graymoor became Roman Catholic, Mother Rosina's questions were no doubt redoubled. By an act of great generosity, the Catholic Church enabled Graymoor to remain as an Order, something that must have eased their transition considerably.

Cyril John Hawes was now Brother Jerome, though he had parted from the Society of the Divine Compassion and had not been able to establish a Community of male Franciscans in Birmingham. He had gone alone to do reconstruction work after a devastating hurricane in the Bahamas, and sharing the doubts of many Anglo-Papalists, wrote to Mother Rosina Mary after the secession of the Society of the Atonement, to be told that Mother Rosina Mary was considering following their example. In the end the majority of the Sisters of the Community of St Francis became Roman Catholics, including a novice who had joined the Community in 1908, and whose personal devotion to Mother Rosina Mary caused her to be called 'the cabin boy'. This close relationship between a Reverend Mother and a novice recurs in the history of the Community of St Francis, and despite all the checks and balances put in place by practical wisdom and the Rule, there were times when the issue of favouritism became acute.

At the time of the conversion of most of the Sisters, however, it should be noted that despite being disowned and disinherited by her family for her conversion, the 'cabin boy' not only accompanied Mother Rosina Mary but persisted in her calling to the Religious Life.

In fact, and again due to the generosity of the Roman Catholic Church and benefactors from the United States of America for the costs, six of the Community of St Francis Sisters were able to be received together into Mother Lurana's Society of the Atonement, after a brief sojourn with some Roman Catholic Sisters in Mill Hill.

As Sister Elizabeth records, in 1910:

Six members of the Community of St Francis arrived in New York on 21 November and were received into the fold of St Peter on the 26th. Mother Rosina Mary changed her name to Sister Mary Magdalene. Annie Margaret became Margaret Mary and Elizabeth Clara changed to Clara Francis. The other three were novices, Teresa, Mary Francis and Angela, the cabin boy! Of the six, only one was eventually life professed at Graymoor, Sister Teresa, who added Francis to her name. In the following January, Sister Mary Magdalene was sent, with one of the original Atonement Sisters, to the Franciscan Missionary Sisters of the Scared Heart at Peekskill, for experience in Catholic novitiate practices. Very quickly she decided that here was her real spiritual home. On 15 January 1911 she entered officially and remained, making Perpetual Vows on 25 July 1919, 35 years after her first consecration at Lloyd Square. The faithful cabin boy followed her to the end, and made her vows as Sister Mary Claudia on the same day. These Franciscan Sisters worked in the care and teaching of children and Sister Mary Claudia was subsequently trained for this work. Sister Mary Magdalene however, 'in her humility requested to be assigned to the menial work of the house' (from letter from Peekskill Sisters). The remaining members of the group who reached Graymoor, all returned to England on different dates in 1911, returning to secular life. (Elizabeth CSF, 1981, p. 18)

All this might be seen as defeat and disaster, but often when I talk with Sister Beverley, she refers to the 'Fourth Order of Franciscans', those who have begun but not persisted in the Life. For Beverley, certainly, there is no defeat or disaster in this but a sense that sometimes God calls people for a time to share in the life of the Community, to give and receive, to grow and to move on. Many of these 'Fourth Order' keep more or less in contact with the Sisters, and many of them were there to celebrate the Community's move from Compton Durville. But that is to pre-empt the later story considerably.

Peekskill Memory

There is a fascinating postscript to Mother Rosina Mary/Mary Magdalene's part in the history of the Community of St Francis. In 2011 some British Sisters of the Community of St Francis were visiting New York for a First Order Chapter and visited Peekskill on a day out. While at the convent of the Sacred Heart, a Sister had just celebrated her 100th birthday, and had been asked to speak to the Community of St Francis Sisters. As she began to speak, prompted by one of her own Community, the Community of St Francis Sisters realized with amazement that she was speaking of their own foundress. This is what was said:

> (Peekskill Sister) *Tell us about Mother Magdalena. Can you tell us anything about her?*
> Well, the one thing I'll tell you about her, is I was scared stiff of her. And she took a liking to me. I used to tremble when she'd want me. But she was a very, very wholesome, good woman after you got to know her. That was just her way. I think she was stationed at our business school in Manhattan.
> *Yes, that's in her record.*
> And then she was here. Oh I remember, she used to have charge of the large parlour, and she had little girls that helped her. Oh, she had those little girls perfect – and they loved her. And she would have them write compositions on good housekeeping.
> Oh, I remember too, when she was 25 years with us, the Sisters gave

her a golden jubilee because she was 28 years with the Anglican Sisters, so they gave her a golden jubilee instead of a 25th anniversary. But she was a wonderful, wonderful person. Wonderful person – good Religious.

Do these people know Sister Claudia? Anybody know who she is? You remember her, right?
Well, she was a postulant with Sister ... well her first name was Sister Rosina ...

... That was Magdalena ...
... but after she was in our community she took the name Magdalene. And Sister Claudia, she was a postulant in England, and she wanted to come with Sister Magdalene but Sister Magdalene wouldn't let her. She thought this is just a schoolgirl crush – I'm not going to spoil your life. Sister Magdalene came to Graymoor and the Cardinal advised them to go through a legitimately established novitiate. And since they were right next door, naturally they came with us. And it was while they were here with us that Sister Magdalene changed to our community instead of Graymoor, and while Sister Magdalene was here, who appeared one day, but Sister Claudia? She was [inaudible] with I forget her family name. So both of them were here in the same band – Sister Magdalene and Sister Claudia. And Sister Claudia had that real Oxford way of speaking and when she was stationed in Philadelphia, they used to say she spoke a foreign language because she had that accent.

They tell about this little child that had Sister Claudia as a teacher, and the first day that she had Sister as her teacher, she went home and her mother asked her, 'How do you like your new teacher?' And she said, 'She's real nice, but she speaks broken English.'
Sister Claudia lived to be a good age. She died in her 70s. I think she was in her 70s. Anyway, it's great to have you [CSF Sisters?] because I feel that I grew up with you. I didn't know you back then. I thought they were all Catholics, even though you don't tell the difference.

3
Companions of the Poor

Day 5

The Master willingly embraced a life of poverty in this world. *He was rich, yet for your sakes he became poor.* (2 Corinthians 8.9)

He chose a stable for his birthplace and for his upbringing the house of a village carpenter. Even that home he left in early manhood and became a wayfarer, with *nowhere to lay his head.* (Matthew 8.20)

Us also he calls to poverty.

Whoever serves me must follow me. (John 12.26)

None of you can become my disciple if you do not give up all your possessions. (Luke 14.33)

The Brothers and Sisters, therefore, seek to be poor in spirit. They desire to escape from the love of the world and the things that are in the world and rather, like their patron Saint Francis, to be in love with poverty. They covet only the unsearchable riches of Christ. They recognise, indeed, that while some of their members may be called to a literal following of Saint Francis in a life of actual penury and extreme simplicity, for most so high an ideal will not be possible.

(Principles Day 5)

The early years of the remnant of the Community of St Francis were committed to living with and among poor people, despite the Revd Charles Thornely's profile of the parish of Dalston. For this parish, poverty often meant destitution, homelessness and hunger for a whole class of society. The years following the Wall Street Crash of 1929 and the global economic depression that followed had devastating effects on those in the so-called lower classes in the UK. By 1933, 25 per cent of the British workforce was unemployed, but even in the early years of the century, poverty was endemic. Like those who had founded the Community, the decision of the remaining Community of St Francis Sisters to remain in Dalston was highly significant theologically as well as politically. Like St Francis, their following of the way of Jesus focused on a recognition that God was to be encountered, and loved, in the poor and desolate, not least those made sick by the untreated diseases of poverty and malnutrition.

Quite what their parishioners thought of the conversion to Roman Catholicism, and departure of two-thirds of the small Franciscan Sisterhood, is not known. There is simply no evidence. Those who remained, though, bravely decided to continue, when, one can only imagine, they might have been tempted to join with some stronger and more established Community. Although it is difficult to imagine that the three Sisters, only one of whom was in life vows, did not consider this, there is no evidence of pressure from the church hierarchy for them to do so.

Sister Elizabeth records:

Father Thornely, their parish priest and chaplain appointed Sister Elizabeth the Mother of the tiny group … she had already shown gifts of leadership and administration at the time of the move from Hull, and again to the larger house. Helen Elizabeth Christmas was by all accounts a formidable woman. A nurse who had worked under her at Guy's hospital, and who later assisted the Community in their nursing home, recalled how in the hospital her reputation as a stickler for discipline evoked the whispered warning as she approached, 'Pst, here comes Christmas!' The Lord added indomitable courage to her strong character. (Elizabeth CSF, 1981, p. 21)

Sister Elizabeth hints, perhaps, though more kindly than Rosalind Essex, at a martinet streak to Mother Elizabeth's character, one that might be contrasted with St Clare's admonition to leader(s) of the Poor Ladies:

Let her [the Mother] also be far sighted and discerning towards her sisters, as a good mother is toward her daughters, and let her especially take care to provide for them according to the needs of each one out of the alms that the Lord shall give. Let her also be so kind and affable that they may securely reveal their needs and confidently have recourse to her at any hour, as they see fit both for themselves as well as for their sisters. (Armstrong, 2006, p. 64)

It is not uncommon in popular culture, as in television programmes like *The Vicar of Dibley* and *Call the Midwife*, to portray women in church leadership as uncongenial, but I read Sister Elizabeth's words alongside her assertions, mentioned above, that the discipline of her early Franciscan days was being not materially different from that which she experienced at home. Obedience for Sister Elizabeth was what one owed parents, as well as others in authority. Yet for many of those who joined Sisterhoods in the nineteenth and early twentieth centuries, and even today, obedience to parents was one of the givens they had to overcome, even defy, in order to become Sisters in the first place. In this light, Clare's Testament or Rule may reflect her own mother, who is believed to have been a woman of considerable piety and devotion. Yet obedience is not how one would describe her responses to the patriarchal demands of her father and male relatives, nor her later passionate demand for 'the privilege of poverty' from the Papacy.

Whatever the case was with Mother Elizabeth, she and her two Sisters received the support of those who might be seen as in authority over them. Not only did their parish priest offer support, but the Rt Revd Cosmo Lang, later Archbishop of Canterbury, then Bishop of Stepney, became their Visitor, and their earlier mentor and supporter the Revd Winnington Ingram continued to offer support. Of them all Mother Elizabeth wrote:

We are overwhelmed when we reflect on their goodness to us at that time! Many ups and downs could be recorded during these years ... The present Community owes its existence to them. (Elizabeth CSF, 1981, p. 22)

Mother Helen Elizabeth.

If obedience is a word to be reinterpreted in the light of the strength of character of these women, and their defiance of convention, the excerpt of the letter above suggests that deference was, at times, more obviously embraced. Nonetheless, it is hard to deny that it is to the persistence of the three Sisters – and who can estimate the 'ups and downs' they experienced – together with the grace of God, that the present Community owes its existence.

Sister Elizabeth again notes the difficulties of managing with such diminished numbers a large House and enterprise which the originally much larger community had embarked upon. Loyalty to the Rule and the Office, did not, however, Sister Elizabeth records, falter:

never did they allow any relaxation or break in their spiritual discipline or in the recitation of the Divine Office. The regular round of prayer and praise became a vital staying power, giving value and meaning to the rest of life. (Elizabeth CSF, 1981, p. 23)

This commitment continues to this day, and echoes Sister Beverley's words to students at the Queen's Foundation about 'prayer on the hoof', rooted in the Office. *The Daily Office SSF*, as used in the Community of St Francis houses I have visited, is indeed a vital staying power, but it also provides an offering of the whole of life to God, and a number of Sisters spoke to me of this emphasis of prayer as integrating the whole of life. I am especially impressed by the way the Sisters at Leicester bring to their prayers of intercession, as well as the wider world and the wider issues of Leicester, those whom they have encountered that day, be it the window cleaner, the mother and toddler they have met in the street, or someone they have met in the course of being a tutor in computing at the local community computer training scheme.

The offering up of daily life and what may seem unimportant in the Daily Office recognizes that all of life belongs to God, and is a place for God's transforming love to be celebrated and longed for. The petition, 'Your kingdom come, Your will be done', is at the heart of Christian prayer, and this longing for the coming of God's reign lies too at the heart of all discipleship and professed Religious Life. For the current members of the Community of St Francis whom I have interviewed, this suggests a consciousness that writers such as Brother Lawrence (*The Practice of the Presence of God*) and Jean Pierre de Caussade (*The Sacrament of the Present Moment*) draw upon, an understanding of discipleship that means all living that is shot through with the values of the kingdom, with generous love, is life addressed to God and, therefore, mysteriously, prayer. This integrative prayer is closely related to a life of poverty in the spirit of Sisters Francis and Clare and of Matthew 25.31–46. As the late Sister Jenny Tee said to me when I was discussing some teaching I had done with student Rabbis at Leo Baeck College, 'What did you say about where we encounter Jesus? I'd have said: "In other people, especially the vulnerable."'

The Privilege of Poverty

Throughout this story are reminders that at the heart of the Franciscan life is a commitment to poverty. In the life of St Francis this commitment was so compelling that he personified poverty, calling her 'the Lady' or 'Lady Poverty'; and using the language of the troubadours of his day, he is portrayed as pursuing her, as a lover pursues the beloved. St Francis goes in search of her, follows where she calls him, is her servant. Although the device of courtly love was common, this devotion to poverty was strange even at the time of St Francis. Why should one love poverty or attend to her call? For St Francis the answer to this was quite simply that it was the call to follow Jesus Christ. In doing so, he turned away from the mercantile class into which he had been born and in which the beginnings of capitalism might be observed, turning instead towards the Christ who had 'nowhere to lay his head' (Matthew 8.20; Luke 9.58), and

> who, though he was in the form of God, did not regard equality with God as something to be exploited, but emptied himself, taking the form of a slave, being born in human likeness. And being found in human form, he humbled himself and became obedient to the point of death – even death on a cross. (Philippians 2.6–8)

St Francis' expression of his devotion to Lady Poverty was to respond to the call to emulate Christ, as he endeavoured to do in all his living and preaching, and he did so in what we may consider rather extreme ways. Some of the most famous narratives of St Francis' life concern this devotion, most notably the story of the young Francis taken by his father, Pietro Bernardone, before the bishop, rightly accused of stealing from his father in order to repair the church (San Damiano), a task to which St Francis believed himself called. St Francis, as the hagiographies tell us, not only promised to repay what he owed but took off his clothes, to symbolize his dependency on God. Here the hagiographies differ: in some he is naked and the bishop covers him with his cloak, in others St Francis is revealed in nothing but a hair shirt. Whichever version is correct, and it is possible that some other account yet is more historically accurate, this story has caught the imagination of many Christians. It has also been regarded as a sign of Francis' madness; but then, from the earliest days of Christianity, the following of Christ has been accounted foolishness (e.g. 1 Corinthians 1.21).

Nonetheless, in the the mainstream of ancient and medieval monasticism, as expressed in the Rule of St Benedict, there is no vow of poverty. Instead, under the rubric of *conversatio morum* (sometimes translated 'conversion of morals', and sometimes understood as 'faithfulness to the monastic life'), this third vow, alongside obedience and stability, is often taken to mean simplicity of life, a rather different emphasis from that of poverty.

St Francis' times are often characterized by the indictment of rich and corrupt clerics, whose concerns are portrayed as far from 'simplicity', let alone the gospel call to follow Jesus in the way of the poor. Yet there were movements other than early Franciscanism which embraced poverty, or at least simplicity in response to this, not least among the heretical and anti-hierarchical movement of the Albigensians, a sect that provided the backdrop to many of the developments in the theology and practice of the Western Church of the time. Within orthodox Christinaity, however, St Francis' stance was not only reforming, it was radical and counter-cultural. Michael Robson hints at a critique of nascent capitalism in Francis' decision to withdraw from his father's business, something that seemed incompatible with gospel values:

> Despite his good resolutions, Francis was so immersed in his commercial activities that his thoughts were focused primarily on his own business and the drive for profit to the detriment of those less privileged. (Robson, 1997, p. 95)

St Francis' attachment to Lady Poverty might be seen, then, as having political and structural implications, as an assertion of the values of the Reign of God, which were and are both highly contentious and yet for some deeply compelling.

I think it is important to make it clear that although St Francis used the 'romantic' language of courtly love to speak of Lady Poverty, Franciscans are not at all romantic about the devastating effects that grinding poverty can have on individuals, communities and societies; indeed in his book on St Francis, to which I have already referred, the Latin American Liberation theologian Leonardo Boff uses the phrase 'for the poor against poverty' (Boff, 1985). Using this phrase as a gospel imperative, Boff explores what Franciscan poverty might mean for disciples today stating clearly that material poverty needs to be abolished.

> One of the marks of poverty is a dependency on others, and those first Sisters at Dalston relied not only on the grace of God and the support of the Church hierarchy, but also on the financial support of a district nurse, Ethel Bannister, who lived with the Sisters at various points during the years 1910–12, putting all her financial resources into the reborn Community and its work. A nascent Anglican Third Order began to develop too, and the Confraternity of St Francis emerged among men as well as women who supported the vocation of the Sisters but were either unable to become members of the community or simply did not feel called to the form of Religious Life which the Sisters inhabited. Support here was prayerful, practical and financial. The vicar of Plaistow contributed, for example, alongside his spiritual and psychological input, two loaves of bread a week. (Elizabeth CSF, 1981, p. 25)

At this point too relations between the early Franciscan male community, then in the form of the Community of the Divine Compassion, and the Community of St Francis began to be important for both groups. The Community of Divine Compassion had a house at that time in Plaistow, where Brothers worked among the very poor of the London slums.

As will be seen, this link between the two Franciscan communities in solidarity with poor people was to continue, not least in closely associated houses where, for example, as in Belfast, they lived in two houses in the same street. There were also to be shared houses at Halcrow Street, Stepney, and Toynbee Hall. In Glasgow, where Sister Moyra CSF lived with Brothers from late 2001 to 2003, the Brothers and Sister all moved to Dundee, where she lived with the Brothers until 2007, sharing again the life of poor communities.

The toughness of this form of Religious Life continued and continues. Like some of the early Beguines, the early Community of St Francis Sisters took in washing as a way of financing their lives in Hull. Sister Elizabeth gives an account of the difficulties of washing at Dalston too, using the letters of Sister Lillian, who entered the Community in 1915:

> To do washing, boiling and rinsing by candlelight has its difficulties. We used to put a bucket upside down on top of the wringer and stand the candlestick on that, but when, as sometimes happened, an unlucky jerk was given, down would come bucket and candle into the tub below. We were all in the dark until the bucket was replaced and a dry candle found. Often while this went on the copper would boil over and *then* we were in a mess which had to be mopped up before we could get on with the job. The drying and ironing room had to be at the top of the house, which meant carrying wet clothes upstairs several times a day, folding them when dry and bringing them down to be mangled before taking them up again to be ironed and packed. The irons, of course, were flat irons, and had to be heated on the stove, cleaned and tested with a drop of water for the right temperature ... (Elizabeth CSF, 1981, pp. 25–6)

This so-called menial work continues to be part of the life of the Community from time to time; so, for example, Sister Beverley in Leicester has for a period earned her living as a church cleaner while fulfilling her priestly ministry in the same parish.

Evidence of the way the early Sisters led deprived lives is given by Sister Elizabeth in a number of stories, among them the association of butter on bread with feast days and other special occasions (p. 24), the special treat for a Eucharistic presider – not the Sisters – of 'One ounce of ham cut thin' (p. 25). She quotes again from Sister Lillian:

> It was war time and we were very poor. We lived on two shillings and sixpence per head per week and usually had meat on Sundays only. Our beds were boards of tresses, the mattresses sacks filled with straw. (pp. 24–5)

At this time, of course, vegetarianism did not have the vogue it does today, even among Franciscans in fraternity and sorority with God's creation; and in the 'brief boom' of 1914–21, the average farm labourer earned the equivalent of £1.70 per week.

As well as the vicar's contribution of bread, the Sisters often made use of donations of stale bread put aside for poor people. Other practical help came from parishioners, who were sometimes able to offer skills and repairs to the fabric of the convent. Miss Elizabeth Boult, a long-standing friend of the community, as well as sister of the conductor Sir Adrian Boult, left the Sisters enough money to install electricity, something which vastly improved their lives, not least in relation to the laundry.

Called to live this life were not only straightforwardly middle-class young women for whom these privations must have been a shock, however voluntarily they entered into the life, but also those facing other challenges. Sister Elizabeth mentions a novice who seems to have survived childhood polio with the aid of leg irons and surgical boots, during this early period, and it should be noted that Sister Elizabeth herself – enormously influential Minster Provincial in a later period of the Community's life – contended and contends with disabilities that must have made her life extraordinarily difficult at times.

Many of the Sisters in the early part of the twentieth century had established and sometimes prestigious jobs before embracing a life of poverty and prayer. Sister Elizabeth records a musician, and Sister Chris, who is currently much appreciated for her work among deaf and deaf/blind people, started her professional life as a children's tailor making clothes for the children of Princess Margaret Rose, among others.

Part of sharing a life of poverty was to be alongside those for whom chronic illness, malnutrition and premature death featured daily, and this perhaps inevitably so in the days before the National Health Service. The recognition of suffering related to illness provoked a development in the Sisters' vocation, namely the establishment of a home for the care of the incurable.

The Religious Life, including that of the Benedictines, had always been characterized by hospitality to those who were sick, and St Francis' own hagiography includes care for those who through the appalling stigma of leprosy were ostracized from society in a way that is reminiscent of the time of Jesus. There is also the very famous story of St Francis leaping from his horse to embrace a leper, to find his embrace returned and on resuming his ride, noticing the leper had disappeared, suggesting that it was Christ under the guise of a leper whom Francis had greeted. As Sister Gillian Clare OSC used to say, 'Francis made a preferential option for the poor because he made an option for Christ.' In addition to this symbolic action, Francis is recorded as frequently engaged in caring for lepers, as his *Testament* records:

> 'When I was in sins, it seemed extremely bitter to me to look at lepers, and the Lord himself led me among them and I practiced mercy with them.' So greatly loathsome was the sight of lepers to him at one time, he used to say, that, in the days of his vanity, he would look at their houses only from a distance of two miles and he would hold his nostrils with his hands. But now, when by the grace and the power of the Most High he was beginning to think of holy and useful things, while he was still clad in secular garments, he met a leper one day and, made stronger than himself, he kissed him. From then on he began to despise himself more and more, until, by the mercy of the Redeemer, he came to perfect victory over himself. (First Life of Francis, 17[4])

In 1919, the neighbours of the Community of St Francis departed and gave their house to the Sisters, who, Sister Elizabeth suggests, were at first bewildered by this generous but demanding gift (Elizabeth CSF, 1981, p. 33). The Sisters' emersion in the community had made the need for nursing care obvious, however, and their work in support of the District Nurse who lived with them, especially in ministering to the dying, presented itself to them after a short time as a call to serve those who were terminally ill, providing a kind of hospice. Making use of equipment made available to them from a military hospital that was being closed, partially restructuring the houses and thoroughly cleaning and polishing the house fell to the Sisters. After a brief fright when it seemed the council

---

4 www.vatican.va/spirit/documents/spirit_20001103_tom-da-celano-en.html.

might take possession of the house because it was unoccupied (p. 32), the Sisters began to sleep there, and thus secured, the home was opened and blessed by the Rt Revd Henry Moseley on St Francis Day, 4 October 1919.

It may well be that the poor of East London did not represent the same level of aesthetic challenge that lepers offered, but nursing the chronically sick was heroic in its own way too, and here the Sisters could offer something that many poor people in the neighbourhood could not offer: time and basic nursing care. This new ministry did not, however, mean that they could abandon the work of the laundry, but was something extra that they took on. It was a development that was to focus the work of the Community of St Francis for generations to come, but did not relieve them of the necessity of earning their living, at least not at first. In this they again shared the life of poor people, who struggled to care for their elderly and sick family and friends while trying to earn enough money to live.

Sister Elizabeth's account is of a period of stability and contentment, and she describes the home as 'always a very happy place, due largely to the sense of humour and optimism prevailing' (p. 32). It was clear from the first that the commitment of the Sisters was to care for patients until they died, unless hospitalization was necessary. In pre-National Health Service days, patients and their families must have been enormously relieved to have found such a refuge and respite from the often overwhelming demands that someone chronically and terminally ill might make on a household, when household tasks were often relentless and there was little, if any, money to spare to help ease inexorable conditions. Sister Elizabeth writes, 'from the first, the pastoral care was considered as important as the physical, and preparation for death a part of the normal business of living' (p. 33). In a way which echoes some of the emphasis of the modern hospice movement, Sister Elizabeth notes the importance of environment and ethos:

> There was a warm family atmosphere and in spite of medical essentials, wards, day room and so on were made as attractive as possible and

daily prayers were a natural not an enforced event. (p. 33)

The gardens of convent and home were amalgamated, and patients were encouraged to be in the garden as much as possible. This must have been balm indeed for those who had lived in crowded and constrained conditions.

The home had 18 beds, divided between three wards – the largest, named St Mary on the first floor, and the two smaller wards, St Clare and St Agnes, on the ground floor. As well as the oversight and professional care of the District Nurse, Ethel Bannister, the home benefitted from the presence of Nurse Barry for some time. Since funds were tight, however, the Sisters were responsible for night duties, though Ethel Bannister was living with them initially, and then just a short walk away, and it is to be imagined that she might be called for any emergencies that did not conflict with her district work.

Sister Elizabeth gives an account of a convivial place, where donations from supporters enabled the purchase of radios, gramophones and even eventually televisions to enable patients to watch the wedding of Princess Margaret. The original Mother Elizabeth encouraged the visits of children, and Sister Elizabeth records visitors: children and adults singing popular songs of the time as well as hymns, to the accompaniment of a piano played by one of the Sisters. Altogether Sister Elizabeth offers a story of considerable fun, of singing and acting and dressing up, not least by the Sisters, for the entertainment of patients. There were outings too, focusing on churches dedicated to St Francis, as well as visits to more celebrated settings.

The impression is given of a light-hearted cheerful life at the home, which also coloured response to things that went awry. There are accounts in *Corn of Wheat* of the pursuit of the convent dog who had discovered a denture; the finding of a poker hidden under a mattress (p. 37) and for Sister Elizabeth these were also redolent of something highly important about the Christian and Franciscan life:

To be God's fool was not beneath St Francis. Laughter, with that sense of proportion that does not take itself too seriously, is of the essence of the Kingdom of God and undeniably an ingredient of the Franciscan mixture. (p. 37)

Other parts of the mixture of life for the Sisters in Dalston were the celebration of very ordinary people and their families who contributed so much to the life of the home and of the Sisters. And of course the professionals: doctors, and especially qualified nurses who were able to offer their particular skills into the business of caring. Sister Elizabeth writes of 'Nurse Bannister, and after the Second World War, Miss Welton, whom all called "Matron" ... continued to give friendship, support and service through the years.' And in tribute to the death of one of these key figures, Sister Elizabeth notes: 'To her as to so many, we owe a debt that could never be paid. Her Lord and ours will complete her sure reward' (p. 39).

It is easy for those of us who live albeit in times of difficulty for the National Health Service to forget the fear and hardship with which so many poor elderly people and their families viewed chronic illness and death. The simple expense of going to see a doctor meant that very many of those who were not wealthy lived with conditions which went untreated, and with sometimes acute pain which would be unacceptable to us now. The Sister's home offered care to those who could not afford to pay for it – the home was mostly funded by donations. The sisters also offered friendship and hope to relatives, and to the neighbourhood and beyond.

Down and Out in London

Britain between the First and Second World Wars was a place of shocking poverty and deprivation, and migrant workers – not from foreign lands but from other parts of the country – found themselves travelling to London in the hope of finding the work that would help support families in the north of England. Many former soldiers had become displaced through lack of work, or the mental health issues that arose from the mismatch between the trenches and family life. When this was exacerbated by poverty and lack of medical understanding, let alone money to fund mental health care, itinerancy was often a result. The demise of so many country estates after the First World War also meant that farm workers found themselves unemployed, and these people often drifted to the cities and especially to London. But work was not necessarily in plentiful supply in London either, and homelessness, alongside poverty, was rife. Here again the Sisters found themselves, like Francis, face to face with the naked Christ, and like Francis they embraced him.

Sister Elizabeth gives the first hint of this in her account of the home, quoting a childhood visitor thus: 'There was a lean-to at the side of the Home where I liked to feed the down and outs …' (Elizabeth CSF, 1981, p. 36). Work with destitute men became a major focus for the Sisters between the wars, alongside the home. The kindness of the Sisters to these poor and often desperate men became known among the growing number of those who sought work in London but discovered that the capital could not provide work for everyone who needed it. Sister Elizabeth notes that 'the convent in Richmond Road soon became known and by 1925 as many as thirty a day were knocking at the door, hopeful for food or clothing' (p. 52).

Franciscanism has been called chaotic and scruffy, and not just by its critics. What this Religious Life 'on the hoof' offers, however, is the potential of enormous flexibility of thinking, and this was brought to bear as the Sisters in Dalston encountered more and more of the men who came to be called 'God's Royalty' (Elizabeth CSF, 1981, p. 52). Thus as the numbers of homeless men at the door of the convent increased, the Sisters saw potential for providing a basic guest house for them, converting the side entrance to the convent, already partially covered. There, as an edition of *The Troubadour* attests:

> Often a few will be seen sewing on buttons or cobbling up a hole. Others, pathetic, weary-looking men will be trying to get some rest on the forms, balancing themselves somehow and resting their heads on their bundles. Some might be fast asleep with their head down

on the table, the picture of dejection. Only those who have seen and talked to men like this have any idea of their wretchedness, and most heartily do we thank all who have sent gifts of money or food or clothing, for some are in dire need. Daily we could recount pathetic stories from conversation with the men, of their real hunger, of the terrible state of their clothing, of the worn and bruised feet, often sockless. To such unfortunates a wash, clean socks and perhaps a clean shirt or a pair of boots is fresh hope. Occasionally they return to tell us of their good fortune if they have found a job; but alas, this is not often, for when men are really 'down and out' and in the pitiable condition that most of these are, it is extraordinarily hard for them to rise at all. Greatly do we rejoice when 'The Floweret' arrives, the monthly paper of the Brotherhood of St Francis, to tell of the things being done in Dorset to give them a chance to recover not only their self-respect but their spiritual vision as well. We beg that all lovers of St Francis will pray for these poor unfortunate brethren, and pray also that we who 'profess and call ourselves Christian' may realise that on us, to a large extent, lies the responsibility of their hopes for the future. (Elizabeth, CSF, 1981, pp. 52–3)

Gradually times were announced for the distribution of food – often hot soup – and clothes also became available, all donated by supporters of the Sisters. Water and soap were available for the washing of bodies and clothes, and eventually an iron coke stove for the men to warm themselves was installed. The Sisters became associated – though not formally so – with the Fellowship of St Christopher, which included the Brotherhood at Batcombe, and the Houses of St Francis set up around the country to provide for homeless and unemployed men. Meanwhile, Sister Elizabeth notes that Mother Elizabeth set up a small confectionary-making business the profits from which supported work among vagrant men. Donations were also received from the people of the neighbourhood, and there is evidence that even the children offered what they could. Numbers of needy men grew, so that at their peak, during the years 1931–32, about 14,000 men made use of the shelter and its facilities. Some of these men, and sometimes women, came back to help the work of the shelter, and sometimes appeared simply to thank the Sisters for enabling them to survive at a very difficult time in life. Occasionally the Sisters were able to help men find housing too.

The work of the shelter came to an end with the outbreak of the Second World War, and although, as will be seen, living with and among poor people was to continue to be a feature of the ministry of the Community of St Francis, as indeed would be the offering of help to wayfarers, the numbers of destitute people finding their way to the Community was not again to reach such proportions.

4
Change but not Decay

Day 20

Jesus the Master took on himself the form of a servant. *He came not to be served but to serve.* (Mark 10.45)

He went about doing good; curing all who were sick; bringing good news to the poor; binding up the broken-hearted. (Acts 10.38), (Matthew 8.16) Those who would claim to be his servants and follow him must be diligent in ministry to others. (Luke 4.18), (Isaiah 61.1)

The active works by which the Brothers and Sisters seek to serve their Master begin within the house and garden. (1 Thessalonians 5.17)

The sweeping, dusting and other menial offices, as well as certain forms of manual work, are apportioned among them so that all may contribute their share to the work of the household and the cost of their own living. All must be capable of engaging in some form of manual work. All must consider the interests of the community in its work for God and study strict economy. Brothers and Sisters will do their own work as far as possible. Saint Francis said that *the idle (member) has no place in the community.*

(Principles Day 20)

In comparison with Mother Helen Elizabeth's long 'rule' of 1910–50, Mother Agnes Mary's 21 years (1950–71) seem short indeed, and yet they saw the community through the aftermath of the Second World War and the development of its future work and identity. This was a difficult time to negotiate, though in many ways not unwelcome, for despite the austerity represented by rationing ending only in 1954, immediately post-war churchgoing seems to have increased in the UK, and the Community of St Francis felt able again to open its novitiate. In addition, many of the social factors that had contributed to widespread poverty, and which had caused hardship for the transient workers, were beginning to be addressed. The foundation of the National Health Service in 1948 had a tremendous effect upon the lives of those who had been at the heart of the ministry of the Community of St Francis. Peter Hennessy quotes Peter Calvocoressi on the significance of this development:

> For its customers it [the NHS] was a godsend, perhaps the most beneficial reform ever enacted in England, given that it relieved so many not merely of pain but of the awful plight of having to watch the suffering and death of a spouse or child for lack of enough money to do anything about it. A country in which such a service exists is utterly different from a country without it. (Hennessy, 1993, p. 119)

The Beveridge Report of 1942 had proposed a system of social security intended to prevent a return of the hardships of the 1930s, and given a commitment to the people fighting and in other ways supporting the war effort. Although the phrase 'a land fit for heroes' dates from the end of the First World War, there is a sense that the government and military hierarchy felt that this time – the end of the Second World War – something must be achieved. In 1946 the National Insurance Act sought to create a system of benefits for people who were unemployed or sick, who were pregnant or elderly. Funded by employees, employers and the government, this offered some fulfilment of the promises made during the war.

It is, nonetheless, difficult to imagine from the perspective of twenty-first century Britain, the lives of ordinary working-class people during the post-war years. Peter Hennessy's book *Never Again* gives some real sense of this time, as does Mike Leigh's film *Vera Drake*, which although focused on the story of abortion, gives a real flavour of the time: cramped conditions, and the limitations of life that seem shockingly 'foreign', except among the very poorest of our time. While I do not in any way wish to

63

undermine the hardship of those who are poor today, and becoming poorer, the prevalence of financial and social hardship characterized so many lives at the end of the Second World War, even when mitigated by a communitarianism often real but sometimes romanticized. In living in Dalston, it was this life that the Community of St Francis shared.

Peter Hennesey, writing of this time, quotes Frank Prochaska's understanding of philanthropy as kindness, based upon his research among working-class communities:

> Philanthropy is defined as love of one's fellow man [sic], an action or inclination which promotes the well-being of others. It is usually studied from the point of view of institutions, but as it implies a personal relationship it is useful to think of philanthropy broadly as kindness. This opens up the subject to include casual benevolence within the family or around the neighbourhood, activities which often expand and lead to the creation of formal societies.
>
> It also helps us to avoid the misconceptions inherent in assuming that charity is invariably a relationship between rich and poor, particularly the view, still current among social historians, that through philanthropic agencies the wealthy simply foster a subservient class of Mr Pooters. Helping others informally is a deep-rooted tradition in Britain, as elsewhere. A necessity in working-class communities, it is widespread among all social classes. It often springs from little more than an impulse, triggered by the needs and aspirations of people who see themselves as part of a community, whether it be the family, the neighbourhood or the nation at large. (Hennesey, 1993, p. 120)

For the Community of St Francis, perhaps, philanthropy might be taken back to its etymological roots, where *philia* is the kind of love between friends, and which recognizes that when Jesus spoke of the love of God, neighbour and self as *agape*, he used *agape* in an all but identical way to the love of friends, *philia*. As Leonardo Boff writes in relation to St Francis and poverty (a text to which I keep returning) the preferential option for the poor may be exercised in a number of ways, including conviviality, sharing the life of poor people as their friends (Boff, 1985, pp. 59–64). The Community of St Francis in its Dalston days can clearly be seen as falling into this category, and its story strongly resonates for me with Prochaska's ideas.

Yet the poor would be always with us, and the post-war period did not produce instant solutions. Homelessness, unemployment, strikes, were also characteristic of this period. As ever the poorest were most vulnerable, and as ever, Franciscans and others were committed to being alongside *il poverello* – the Word who became flesh – and his Brother Francis.

The world, however, was to change very swiftly, so a mere 12 years after the end of the Second World War, in his famous speech of July 1957, Prime Minister Harold Macmillan observed:

> let us be frank about it – most of our people have never had it so good. Go around the country, go to the industrial towns, go to the farms and you will see a state of prosperity such as we have never had in my lifetime – nor indeed in the history of this country.[5]

The world had changed – and even if not prosperous for everyone – there did appear to be significantly more prosperity. The arts, not least novels and the theatre, were celebrating working-class life, and certain sorts of working-class men in particular were being regarded as heroes. John Osborne's play *Look Back in Anger* premiered in 1956 and in many ways the epitome of this movement, was celebrated, though feminist scrutiny might have offered a different verdict.

The world, however, had not changed all that much for some, and elderly and chronically sick people were still in need of the love that recognized in them the face of Christ. To them the Community of St Francis continued to respond, and this lay behind one of the most significant changes of the Community's life – the removal of the Community from London to Somerset, from Dalston to the hamlet of Compton Durville, just outside South Petherton. Apart from a short sojourn in Hull, the Community had been based in the capital, had focused its life among the

---

5 news.bbc.co.uk/onthisday/hi/dates/stories/july/20/newsid_3728000/3728225.stm.

urban poor, the elderly, chronically sick and those who became itinerant in search of work. I can only imagine the wrench this move to the country must have represented. The dominence of the idea of choice is, I believe, overrated in the twenty-first century, or at least it is a luxury not available to many people, especially those who are poor. In embracing a life of poverty the Community of St Francis, under the leadership of Mother Agnes Mary, shared this characteristic of that life, and had no choice but to move from Dalston.

Following the Second World War, there was a significant shortage of housing, despite the erection of 'Prefabs': small prefabricated one-story homes that were quickly produced as some of Britain's industrial war resources were redirected. Three hundred thousand were built, intended to last for ten years, though some are still treasured homes today. At the same time there was a programme of slum clearance in London and other major cities, and it was this of which the home and convent in Dalston fell foul.

The clearance of what was considered inadequate housing, with poor or no plumbing, was intensified after the Second World War, though because of the logistics of rehousing people, demolition and then building, this was a tremendous venture. And there were many worse places than Dalston. In fact it was not until 1956 that there was even a hint of demolition coming to Dalston, though that year the houses opposite both the convent and home were demolished. Sister Elizabeth gives an account (p. 75) of the double-bind in which the Community of St Francis found itself, at once under pressure to improve its facilities and nursing standards and at the same time denied the permissions required for the former because of the plans for demolition.

The Sisters looked at several possibilities for an alternative location in and around London, but to no avail. Then their friend the Revd Paul Corin, in whose Hackney Wick parish the first Branch House had been established – of which more in Chapter 5 – moved to Ealing, where a large clergy house would be available, and plans were begun by an architect for extensions and adaptations to accommodate patients and the growing convent. Problems grew, however, because of the joint ownership of the property by the diocese and the Church Commissioners. Permissions for 'change of use' failed to reach the promised agendas, and, as Sister Elizabeth puts it, 'one problem after another seemed to rear up'. Finally, there were issues with the right of way for dustbin collection and:

> By some intuition this was the last straw for Mother Agnes Mary. She had the habit of struggling in thought and prayer when any important decision was to be made and in this case had been unable to feel convinced about the matter in spite of many positive indications, and in the absence of any other offers. News of the dustbin entrance delay suddenly gave her a clear negative and she acted immediately. A Sister passing the door was called in to Mother's Office and asked to wait while a letter was finished and to take it to the post. 'We're not going to Ealing,' said Mother. (Elizabeth CSF, 1981, p. 76)

In the meantime, the Sisters of the Society of the Sacred Cross moved from the Manor House at Compton Durville, and returned to their Mother House at Tymawr, and in due course as the demolition of the Dalston Houses grew ever closer, the Brothers of the Society of St Francis alerted Mother Agnes Mary to the availability of the House at Compton Durville. By now Father Charles SSF was the Warden of the Community of St Francis. He was reported as being very direct, and 'a very firm advisor'! The decision was not easy, however, for, as Sister Elizabeth puts it: 'The Sisters voiced fears of leaving the London area and all their roots, fears of being cut off in the wilds of the west country, fears of the effect on our work and out new-found growth; and Mother Agnes Mary was afraid of cows' (p. 76)!

There were advantages, however, and, in any case, courage is a notable virtue in Religious Life.

There were also some interesting Franciscan links with the Manor House at Compton Durville. After the Society of the Sacred Cross Sisters left it in 1959, the Fidelity Trust – to whom it had been given by Charles Firth in the hope it would be a Religious House – were unable to find another Religious Community to live there. It was, therefore, proposing that the house be returned to Firth's widow. She was a niece of James

Adderley, the Co-Founder of the Society of the Divine Compassion, and while the house was put on the market for possible rental, Father James began to promote it as a home for the Community of St Francis and its patients.

Sister Anne had taken her holiday at Compton Durville in 1959, while the Society of the Sacred Cross Sisters were still in residence, and had reported an enthusiasm for all but the chiming of the clock. Father Charles promoted the advantage of being only 20 miles from the Brothers of the Society of St Francis, and eventually Mother Agnes Mary and Sister Veronica went to see the house. They recognized that adaptations would need to be made, especially for the establishment of a home.

Commitment to their patients meant that it was intended to house any of the patients from Dalston who wanted to move. It is not clear whether the patients were consulted but one imagines Somerset might have been attractive for those who had survived poverty and war in London. At first it was hoped that the Manor's stable block might be converted into a nursing home, but this proved impossible, and as demolition orders were served on home and convent in Dalston, the decision was made to go ahead with the move, and, temporarily, to house patients on the first floor of the Manor House, while the necessary building work took place.

Helped enormously by two major appeals, over two years, via the BBC's *Week's Good Cause*, money was found for the adaptations, but in the meantime, the move was arranged. Sister Elizabeth's account of the move, in which she took part, gives a real flavour of the events, and so I quote her at length:

> On August 1st 1962, the advance guard west to Compton Durville. Furniture vans arrived soon after breakfast and were loaded up with remarkable speed. Everything went from the Convent and a good deal from the Home, leaving only absolute essentials for the patients and mattresses on the floor for the Sisters remaining.
>
> Sister Gabriel wrote: 'At eleven a.m. our kind friend Mr William Webb arrived with his car, which was soon loaded with Mother, Sister Lillian, now over ninety, and me: our luggage, food stores

and one budgerigar in a cage. We had a very good run down, every mile increasing the sense of anticipation, and arrived at Compton Durville at four o'lock. Quickly we went into our new Convent, which, although quite empty except for a table and a few chairs in the refectory and three beds upstairs, had a warm welcoming feel. Apart from the fact that my bed collapsed before I could lie down on it and I slept on the floor, all had a good night. Sister Lillian by virtue of her superiority of age, had a garden chair added to the furniture of her room. Our good friend Mrs Firth took us to Mass at Shepton Beauchamp and having had tea out the day before, we came back to our first meal in the Convent, breakfast in the sunny refectory.

'Soon the furniture vans arrived and began to unload, and for the rest of that day and the following, the unloading went on almost non-stop. We had not realised how much furniture there was at Richmond Road and how spacious those houses must have been. Towards the end of the second day the Convent was full to bursting and the cellar and barn piled high with beds, chairs, trunks, cupboards and chapel furnishings. The next few days were occupied with getting straight and as near ready as could be for the patients and Sisters. A working party came over from the friary, including Brother Anselm and David Hunt. They were of inestimable help in laying linoleum, putting in wall-plugs and shifting heavy furniture – all very cheerfully, through some of the wettest days of the year.

'Back in London the rest of us worked hard to get thirteen old ladies packed up and ready to move. On August 8th we were up at four a.m., said the Office and breakfasted in the kitchen, washed the patients and gave them their breakfast. At six a.m. came a ring at the door bell and there were six L.C.C. [London County Council] ambulances drawn up outside. The ambulance men were superb and, having plenty of room, helped us pack extra blankets and pillows in the last vehicle, the kind with seats. Only two or three of the patients could walk at all, seven were completely bedridden and travelled as stretcher cases, but they were all as excited as children going on a excursion and in spite of many discomforts during the day, kept very bright and cheerful. One, who was to travel practically flat, insisted on wearing hat and gloves! The patients had been given the option of other places in London but most of them wanted to come with us. Only one was too ill and had been hospitalised a fortnight earlier; and we had not replaced those who died after we were certain of moving.

'Bill Webb was to come again later in the morning for the rear-guard which comprised, as he put it, 'three more Sisters and another bird!' but meanwhile we set off in the ambulances, surprising astonished and sometimes horrified looks on the faces of London's millions on their way to work. Our train was due to leave Waterloo at nine a.m., and we were fortunate to be an hour early as the ambulances had to park a long way from the train and there was only one trolley available for our use. Sections of the rear carriage had been reserved, two stretcher cases to a compartment and we were finally loaded and comfortable with just a minute or two to go. The journey was uneventful and it was a beautiful sunny day so we relaxed, reserving our strength for the other end – and we needed it! By a misunderstanding only one ambulance arrived; and contrary to our expectations the carriage was not to be disconnected, but unloaded as quickly as possible. Luggage and blankets were thrown out onto the platform. Seven stretcher cases and six disabled patients were hurriedly moved amid much laughter and with help from Yeovil Junction staff, who remembered that day for a long time. A last check was made to ensure that all was removed, and the train moved out only ten minutes behind schedule.

'There followed a wait of two or three hours on a hot August afternoon, patients on their stretchers on the platform or sitting on the blankets and pillows, while the ambulance service re-organised to find two more vehicles. The first took four stretcher cases, the next three, while the others all squeezed into the last. Sisters and luggage filled up the space in between. The men were marvellous and the last nine miles uproarious with mirth.'

Sister Gabriel's account takes up the story, 'From midday onwards we were on the qui vive. Sister Lillian stayed near the front door with a Union Jack ready to wave in welcome. Once we saw an ambulance coming down the lane and all sprang to "Action Stations" but it simply drove by without stopping. At last the convoy did come in sight, only three ambulances for all our patients and Sisters! They arrived packed like sardines and somewhat exhausted by their unusual experience but in very good heart, and were soon established in the makeshift wards which were to be their home for the next eighteen months.

'To mark the place as a Franciscan residence open to all we placed on the low wall by the Manor steps a small stone of Francis, sculpted and given by Father Pollock of St Francis, Isleworth, to replace the garden one at Dalston which had been broken. Here the little saint stands, with arms wide in welcome.' (Elizabeth CSF, 1981, pp. 78–80)

Vatican II

If Mother Agnes Mary's legacy was most obviously the consolidation of the Community and the move to Compton Durville, there were other important developments over which she presided, many resulting from the changes in Religious Life that emerged from the Second Vatican Council.

The Decree concerning the Religious *Perfectae Caritatis*, like the rest of Vatican II, was 'to invoke a new Pentecost'. John J. McEleney SJ, writing in one of the two major editions of the Vatican II Decrees, notes in his preface its 'ardent desire of enabling the Church in an ever more perfect manner to live as the Bride of Christ' (Abbott, 1965, p. 462) suggests a Pentecost, a renewal of particular application to those in Religious Life. One of the clear focuses of Vatican II's response to Religious Life was contextualization and charism; that is, a focus on the original charism and calling of each Order, and its contextual interpretation. As McEleney puts it, there was an encouragement 'to reflect seriously and actively so as to discover how their institute could and should be adapted ever more perfectly to the continuously changing circumstances of their own times' (Abbott, 1965, p. 462).

Given the nature of the common Religious vows of poverty,

celibacy and obedience,' it is not surprising that poverty was a key to the understanding of this renewal, but Walter Abbott's summary seems explicitly to echo a Franciscan focus: 'They [Religious Sisters and Brothers] imitate Christ the virgin and the poor man.' And though it is clear that here he means Jesus Christ, *il poverello* – the name given so often to Francis – must surely have resonated in the mind of his readers. Renewing and reframing the Religious vows in the light of the gospels was core to the work of the Council. As the Decree itself states:

> The manner of living, praying, and working should be suitably adapted to the physical and psychological constitution of today's religious and also, to the extent required by the nature of each community, to the needs of the apostolate, the requirements of a given culture, the social and economic circumstances anywhere, but especially in missionary territories. (Abbott, 1965, p. 470)

Religious Life in the UK was so dominated by the Roman Catholic Orders that much of what was learned from the discussions of *aggiornamento* inevitably became examined in, and sometimes embraced by, Anglican Communities. For the Community of St Francis this included the rewriting of the Rule both in response to Vatican II but also to the growing together of a familial relationship between the Community of St Francis and the Society of St Francis. Father Charles SSF, Warden of the Community of St Francis for ten years, died in 1964 and was replaced by Father Oswald, and it was he and Father Hugh SSF who assisted in the significant change of focus for the Community of St Francis. The Rule of St Clare, though always of significance for the history and charism of the Community, was replaced by something that was adapted to reflect the life of the Community of St Clare, and embraced also the *Principles* of the Society of St Francis (see Appendix). Despite Father Hugh's assumption that, as Sister Elizabeth puts it, 'we, being women, would require more specific detail in certain areas' (Elizabeth CSF, 1981, p. 84), the Community was determined to maintain its independence, and adapted and revised Father Hugh's drafts. The Sisters adopted the *Principles* and, I would suggest, in effect became Franciscan Friars.

This was not, however, quite as straightforward as it might seem, and there was a debate about whether as women, albeit apostolic women, the Sisters were in fact the Second Order of St Francis, rather than like the Brothers, First Order. At this stage in the Community's history, identification with the First Order made much more sense, in part because they seemed to be adapting First Order *Principles*, and had always eschewed the enclosure of the Second Order, even while adopting St Clare's Rule. Highly significantly, however, Anglican Franciscanism now had its own Second Order, the Community of St Clare, living in Freeland, Oxfordshire, and which did embrace enclosure, identifying primarily as a Contemplative Order, though as Franciscan contemplatives their commitment to poverty was central, and meant that their life was materially, and in other ways, very tough indeed.

The Community of St Francis continued to be deeply committed to prayer, including the prayer of contemplation, and though they did not use the words, they identified as a 'mixed' community, apostolic and contemplative at once, depending upon the ministries and the discernment of God's will for the community and its Sisters. Like the Society of St Francis, the Community was to find inspiration and direction in St Francis' Rule for Hermits, and as well as producing its own hermits, this enabled those called to a Religious Life focused more closely on a life of prayer to find a place in the Community. More of this will emerge later.

Sister Elizabeth records other changes too, not least in the saying of the Divine Office, where adaptations were made that were more practical for those away from Compton Durville, perhaps on mission with the Brothers, not least the use of the Book of Common Prayer for morning and evening prayer.

Changes, slight at first, were also made in the Sisters' habit, which until that time was:

> ankle length, with long sleeves and a nine-inch turned-back cuff, wimples worn with wide collars, scapulars hanging loose outside the rope and a long veil secured on a buckram hood which must hide the profile! We took up the hems – they didn't get so wet walking

muddy lanes: scapulars were put under the rope and cuffs and veils shortened – that made for less flapping and was less cumbersome in work situations: and an example of Mother Agnes Mary's promptness when changes were needed was shown in respect of our great hoods. One day the Warden, during a telephone conversation, told her that a Sister from another Community had been run over and killed and that at the inquest it was suggested that she probably could not see properly when crossing a road. Immediately Mother acted. Hoods were cut back to a mere off-the-face frame … (Elizabeth CSF, 1981, p. 86)

When Sister Elizabeth was Minister Provincial, wimples were abandoned altogether, and in time veils became a matter of individual choice, the habit was redesigned to be more informal, and was not always worn. Post Vatican II, other culturally specific practices were also brought up to date:

Various customs, some of which were simply outdated social impedimenta and the formalities of the Victorian and Edwardian era, were dropped. A certain spontaneity, or was it merely Franciscan chaos, gradually replaced the 'law of the Medes and Persians'. We no longer lined up waiting for Mother's hand-clap before going into meals – there was nowhere to line up! The curtsey was dropped; it was no longer considered unseemly to cross one's feet; and chatter at recreation, usually in the garden, happened naturally and in groups, the Community being too big for the single conversation centred on the senior present. (Elizabeth CSF, 1981, p. 86)

Particular Friendships

Forward looking in many ways, Mother Agnes Mary's time in office was also marked by a degree of favouritism that made Religious Life difficult and caused frustration for some. There are tales of Sisters being ignored on a daily basis, while others were almost courted by 'Mother'. There are shades of Mother Rosina Mary's 'cabin boy' here, but in a world where 'particular friendships' were frowned upon for their divisive nature, and so that Community life could be truly shared and communal, Mother Agnes Mary's flouting of the rules that she herself had power to interpret with particular authority, must have, and my interviewees tell me did, cause some resentment and unhappiness. From the perspective of the twenty-first century, one has some sympathy for her, and close friendships even in Religious Communities are not now frowned upon, as long as they are not seen as exclusive and the treatment of all is regarded as fair. Mother Agnes Mary probably needed the warmth and affection of particular Sisters to help her bear the leadership of the Community in a time of rapid transition, but there were other Senior Sisters in the Community who might perhaps more appropriately have been her friends and advisors. As it was, when, after 50 years of Religious Life and 21 as Superior, Mother Agnes Mary decided to stand down, she made it known that she had a preferred successor, a Sister very young in the Religious Life. When the election was held, Sister Elizabeth, one of the Seniors, was the other candidate, and was duly elected. Mother Agnes Mary was disappointed, but Sister Elizabeth continued to hold Mother Agnes Mary in high affection.

Obedience Revisited

I have already noted how intolerable 'mindless obedience', as she describes it, was for Rosamund Essex, and how relatively easy it was for Sister Elizabeth, and how the Rule under Mother Agnes Mary was interpreted very differently from the time of Mother Helen Elizabeth. The legacy of Vatican II produced further reform, with its emphasis on the business of listening: to God, to context, to individuals, and especially, in a liberationist way, to the voices of those silenced and silent.

For the most part, then, the Sisters and former Sisters to whom I have spoken have talked of obedience in terms of its Latin roots, *oboedientia*, 'listen to' or 'pay attention to'. And for the most part, at least since Vatican II, that listening has much more been seen as the wisdom of the whole community, not that of an isolated Superior, and all through the guidance of the Holy Spirit.

Much of the focus of obedience in the Community of St Francis' recent past has been a requirement, sometimes accepted as necessary, to go to places that seemed uncongenial, or to be with Sisters who would not necessarily have been chosen companions. Much of this has been met with a generosity of spirit or simple fortitude that recognizes that life does not offer unrestrained choices for many people. For others there is a stronger sense of a theological and spiritual discipline, the cost of discipleship. In this respect a number of Sisters and former Sisters have referred to the prayer of the Methodist Covenant Service as a source of inspiration or a hermeneutical framework for their understanding of obedience:

> I am no longer my own but yours
> Put me to what you will,
> rank me with whom you will;
> put me to doing, put me to suffering;
> let me be employed for you or laid aside for you,
> exalted for you or brought low for you.
> Let me be full, let me be empty,
> let me have all things, let me have nothing.
> I freely and wholeheartedly yield all things
> to your pleasure and disposal.

Sandra Schneiders, Professor Emerita in the Jesuit School of Theology at the Graduate Theological Union in Berkeley, California, and member of the Roman Catholic Immaculate Heart of Mary Order, recognizes in her pivotal work *Selling All* that 'The two vows of community life, poverty and obedience, admit of enormous variety of interpretation among Orders.'

As indicated in Schneiders' work, vows are linked with virtue, the outcome of God's building of character through the formation of disciples, and also the formative practices of Religious Life itself. Where alongside poverty, of a spiritual nature, enhanced by the voluntary embarking of at the very least simplicity, came the virtues of 'humility, obedience, courage and chastity'.

These vows Schneiders interprets most helpfully, using the language of poetry and prophesy:

Words like *poverty* and *obedience* are not literal descriptions, much less prescriptions, of juridical obligations ... They are world-creating metaphors that are hyperbolic in the linguistic tradition of the biblical merism. They intend by their literally impossible extravagance (who can be absolutely poor?) to capture the totality of the commitment being expressed. Hyperbole is exaggeration for effect, the use of extreme language to evoke what is beyond expression. (Schneiders, 2001, p. 108)

Obedience, then, might be the expression of the inexpressible, the apotheosis of the kataphatic tradition. For St Clare, as has been seen, this hyperbole was something to be embodied, as far as possible, in a life of extravagant poverty. I believe there is also something implied in Schneiders' words, which suggests that the life of the Body of Christ – the Church – is equally impossibly, to embody the life of the Trinity. Obedience is, I would suggest, about the ineffable, the explosive eruption that results from seeking to contain what is uncontainable. It is perhaps possible to glimpse this in the work of artists like Juliet Hemmingray or Yvonne Bell, who represent Christian symbols like the cross, or the Eucharistic vessels, exploding with the riches of God's grace. The cross situated in the main quadrangle at the Queen's Foundation for Ecumenical Theological Education, in Birmingham, symbolizes the Christina faith as it disintegrates in the power of the Spirit.

Schneiders goes on to assert the prophetic nature of a vowed life:

The vows are also prophetic language ... It [prophecy] is about identifying what is death-dealing in the culture and calling it into question by publically lamenting the injustice and violence of the system, evoking the memory of God's promises, and animating hope for an alternative future. Prophecy calls into question the claim of the oppressive powers that the status quo is the only possible way for reality to exist and function and announces that in the Reign of God things can and will be different. Justice, especially for the poor and the marginalized, will be realized. (Schneiders, 2001, p. 109)

At times the practices of formation in Religious Life can seem petty: and there was sometimes considerable discomfort for some when in the Community of St Francis attempts were made to create uniformity in the minutiae of life. At one time more senior Sisters were required to report, for example, on the washing-up skills of novices. There were also practices, regarded as somewhat esoteric or eccentric by those outside the Life, like the Chapter of Faults where Sisters were required to 'accuse' themselves of various failings and say sorry, a practice that might also be seen as rather psychologically mature, and an undercutting of any temptation to self-delusion.

Whatever the pettinesses or esotericism, the prophetic aspects of Religious Life, about which Schneiders is so eloquent, has managed to persist and endure through the history of the Community of St Francis. Some Sisters see this in terms of small counter-cultural practices like eating together, living as a 'family'. Other practices have included showing solidarity with neighbours through lobbying for small but significant changes, like persuading the council to change the priority of traffic lights to help pedestrians. Prophetic actions large and small, regarding nuclear weapons, women priests, climate change and many others have featured in the lives of many of the Sisters, and had some public effect, because the press finds Sisters and Brothers in habits at demonstrations irresistible.

5
Compton Durville and Beyond

Day 21

Outside the special works of service to the community itself there are many opportunities of ministry, particularly to the uncared-for, the sick, the suffering and needy. The community sets before it, as the special programme of service which it would like to be able to carry out, those acts of mercy the doing of which even to the humblest the Master declares that he will accept as done unto himself. By helping in the relief of poverty we may give him food and drink.

By hospitality to strangers we may take him in. By relieving those homeless and naked we may clothe him. By caring for the sick we may relieve him. By visiting the prisoners we may cheer him. (cf. Matthew 25.35–45)

The community does not, indeed, expect ever to have at its disposal many funds for the administration of charitable relief, but it will gladly lend its members in the work of such relief and co-operate with others who are doing it. In all such work, the community will seek to serve all irrespective of creed, offering its services not as a bribe but as a reflection of the love of Christ himself.

(Principles Day 21)

The move from London to Compton Durville established a new pattern of working. The focus on the home was paramount, but fairly swiftly in 1967 and after further building work, the Barn Guest House was opened, a key focus of the ministry of hospitality among those seeking rest or retreat. At first a small enterprise, this was to become more significant as years passed, as was some of the Sisters' involvement with retreat-giving among the Third Order and for other groups, and the ministry of spiritual direction.

Provision for rest and retreat has become a vitally important aspect of the work of most of the Anglican Religious Communities, and the First Orders – both Community and Society of St Francis – and indeed Second Order of St Francis, the Community of St Clare at Freeland, continue to enable this, asking a modest donation only in return. Since the 1970s there has been in the Church of England, and other denominations, an increasing emphasis on going on retreat, and the vision of 'a spiritual director for everyone' emerged from an increasing emphasis on the importance of lay people as disciples. Again this was formalized and given impetus by Vatican II. It should be noted, however, that particularly within the more Catholic parts of the Church of England, these two things had been encouraged for many years and not least by the legacy of Evelyn Underhill, who modelled the possibility of lay women as spiritual directors and retreat-givers. Nonetheless, this was often seen as a rather restricted and elite set of practices. Even some lay people seem to believe that these things are 'really only for the clergy'.

Alongside this development at Compton Durville, and as numbers of Sisters grew, there was an increasing emphasis on Branch Houses. The first of these, towards the end of the Community of St Francis' time at Dalston, had begun in the parish of St Mary at Eton. The first branch House was part of one of the nineteenth-century 'settlements' sponsored by universities or public schools, in this case by Eton College. The Eton Mission as it was called was a large enterprise to provide care and support for the poor people in their vicinity. The church was huge, 'of cathedral proportions', notes Sister Elizabeth (Elizabeth CSF, 1981, p. 74), and the vicarage too was unimaginably large by today's standards: Elizabeth notes its having 40 rooms! The young men of Eton College, and others, visited the parish as a kind of 'exposure and experience programme'.

Initially at the Revd Paul Corin's request, the Sisters allocated to work at St Mary's commuted there by bus, but among the generous provision of accommodation was a house meant for a woman parish worker, with five bedrooms, and the Sisters were able to adapt that into a house for Religious. After Paul Corin's retirement, the Sisters stayed on and worked in the Parish under the new incumbent, the Revd Edwin Stark, Sister Francis Mary continuing her parish work for 20 years. When Stark moved to Falmouth, the by then elderly Sister went with him in order to continue the parish work to which she was devoted.

After the move to Compton Durville, and with a growing number of Sisters, the Community began to respond to other requests for help. The archives give accounts across the years of the receipt of many such requests from parishes, and occasionally dioceses. The Community of St Francis Chapter, which more and more shared the Superior's leadership task, fell into a pattern of prayer and analysis of the requests against its charism and the skills and availability of Sisters. Undoubtedly, not least as the community expanded, the Branch House experience offered opportunities for Sisters who were more suited to life with a few others and perhaps in a more unban setting than the focus in Somerset. Others found being away from 'home' less congenial, but, as has been observed in the previous discussion of the vow of obedience, that vow meant accepting, and if possible embracing, a given task and place as if a gift from God. Obedience for the Chapter meant listening for the voice of God, and though often responding in challenging and creative deployment, it tried to consider also the flourishing of individual Sisters, with more or less success.

This work away from Compton Durville, together with the growing Community, raised issues of finance. It was not simply buildings that needed to be maintained, and increasingly Sisters had professional qualifications. For obvious reasons, nurses were drawn to the Community, but it was never primarily a nursing order, like the Community of St John the Divine, for example. Sisters in the new Branch Houses were often at least minimally supported by the parishes that invited them to share their work. Like the Brothers, though, Sisters sometimes began to earn their living, usually in jobs that were part-time, in order to allow time for prayer and ministry, but which made a real contribution to the finances of the Community. This continues to be a major source of income for a Community that will not accept 'dowries', and so both paid work and pensions are of high importance.

Laying the foundation stone, Compton Durville, 1964.

As the Community and Society grew closer together, so the Brothers also began to request the support of Sisters in a number of their parishes and projects in the UK and also abroad. Some of these projects are highlighted in the next chapters, but it should be noted here that Anglican Franciscans were truly pioneering in this work. While some expected scandal to be caused when Brothers and Sisters lived together, in at least one project where for a time one Brother and one Sister lived and worked together, those among whom they lived, knowing little of Religious Life or its vows, simply assumed the two were a married couple.

At first, however, Sisters who worked with the Brothers lived in separate houses, and so it was in Plaistow, where both the Society and the Community were to have a long and continuing relationship. In 1967 – towards the end of Mother Agnes Mary's leadership – the Brothers were expanding their mission from the usual pastoral care of a parish, and associated work, to living a life that owed something both to the Catholic Worker's movement and the inspiration of Dorothy Day and

Peter Maurin, and to the Worker Priests movement that was nascent in the Anglican Church. Here was a model of Religious Life as presence, but presence in unexpected places; and also a model of engagement, opened up by relationships with the neighbourhood and workplace, and including the making of supportive alliances as community development groups emerged. Perhaps too this model of a life of poverty enabled the Community and Society of St Francis to span Leonardo Boff's categories of a convivial living together with poor people and 'fighting for the cause of liberation, searching for ways of overcoming poverty toward more just and participatory forms of work and social life' (Boff, 1982, p. 57). In Plaistow two Sisters from the Community of St Francis moved into a flat at the end of the street where the Brothers were living. One Sister, a Deaconess, was trained as a dental hygienist, and worked as such – half-time – at the then London Hospital. The other Sister worked as a nursing assistant and then in the social services department of the borough council.

Novices, 1970.

The development of Branch Houses necessitated changes to the statutes of the Community of St Francis, and by 1977, under the leadership since 1971 of Sister Elizabeth as Mother, there was set out a means of accountability and governance, which included the election of a Guardian for each House and a local Chapter. In the heyday of the Community of St Francis, Branch Houses were usually required to consist of at least four Sisters, except in special circumstances when a Sister might be associated and accountable to another House. This localization of authority also allowed for the Rule to be interpreted as local ministry allowed. The Statutes passed on Epiphany 1977 included the following clauses:

> 7 The ordering of the day in any House may be varied from time to time as occasion shall require, but shall always be such as to provide opportunity for prayer, study and service, including manual work. Silences shall be observed in each House according to local custom. Each House may draw up for insertion in its Customary a list of days of special observance. On certain of these, and on Sundays, there may be a relaxation of the silence and from manual work and study.
>
> 8 The daily timetable of the House shall be decided by the Guardians in consultation with the local Chapter. The daily timetable shall be included in the Customary and approved by the Sister Provincial.
>
> 9 Each Convent or Friary may choose Spiritual Directors, Confessors and Counsellors from outside the Community for those Sisters who wish to avail themselves of their ministry.
>
> 10 The members of any household shall regard themselves as a family and always endeavour to live, as St Francis desired them to, in Brotherly (sic) love.

This flexibility continues to this day, so that at the Leicester House, where – following the death of Sister Jenny Tee – Sisters Beverley and Chris James live, morning prayer and evening prayer are said together, and usually include any visitors. Midday prayer is said by whoever is in the House, and normally Compline is said together at a time that differs according to the evening activities of the Sisters.

As can be seen from the above, a flexible response to circumstances can settle into a new tradition for a particular context, and what the Statues describe as the 'Customary' reflects that. But over the years Customaries could change – as could Statutes, though the former much more easily than the latter – and reflect changed circumstances and changed emphases, while always maintaining the saying of the Office as paramount. The Convent of St Francis at Compton Durville, which was never quite regarded – at least officially and by the Sisters – as the 'Mother House', produced a Customary, which it is believed dates from the early 1980s, probably before 1983, a Customary that was not quite paralleled elsewhere because of the demands of regular work outside the House in the Branch houses.

The Community of St Francis
St Francis' Convent Compton Durville
Customary Timetable

Mon-Sat
6.00 Call
6.30 Angelus, Prayer Time
7.00 Morning Prayer
7.30 Eucharist Breakfast (Silent)
8.30 Reading of the Rule
Chapter of Faults
Conference
10.30–10.45 Coffee Break

Angelus
12.00 Angelus, Midday Office
12.45 Lunch (Silent)
1.45–2.30 Recreation
4.00 Tea
5.00 Evensong, Intercessions
(excluding Saturday)

Angelus
5.30 Prayer Time
7.00 Supper
7.45–8.00 Hot Drink
9.15 Compline

Sun
6.30 Call
7.00 Morning Prayer
7.30 Eucharist Breakfast
10.30–10.45 Coffee
12.00 Angelus, Midday Office
12.45 Lunch
1.45 Hot Drink
4.00 Tea
5.00 Evensong, Intercessions
5.30 Prayer Time
7.00 Supper
7.45-8.30 Recreation
8.30 Compline

Cross Prayers are said after Evensong on Fridays
The Sunday Gospel is read after Evensong on Saturdays

Quiet and Silence
Silence is kept from after Compline until Conference the next morning (until Breakfast on Sundays). If conversation is necessary it should be brief and quiet. During the day people's needs for a quiet space should be considered, especially in the areas near Sisters' rooms, outside the chapels and in the library.

Quiet Days and Days Off
It is the custom of this House for each Sister to have an Individual Quiet Day each month and when possible a Day Off each month.

Study
Each Sister is required to spend a minimum of three hours each week in study to facilitate spiritual growth.

Abstinence
Days of abstinence are kept according to the Church's rule.

House Meeting
A meeting of all the Sisters in this House takes place at least once every two months. This meeting gives more leisure for discussing points held over from Conference, the results of a Chapter meeting or items of common interest or concern.

Branch Houses Accounts and Reports

Toynbee Hall

These were pioneering times and embraced an exciting opportunity at Toynbee Hall, which included Sisters and Brothers living together. In East London, on Brick Lane, Toynbee Hall has a long history as a place of Christian mission and ministry. Founded in 1884, it was the first of the London Settlements, by the late 1970s providing living accommodation for students and young people needing particular support. In 1978 there was a large population of people of Bengali heritage living in the area, and there were tremendous language difficulties, especially for women, and this affected their heath and medical well-being. There were in 1978 two Bengali-speaking GPs but they were both men, and so women would not go to see them.

Sister Leonore – MBE.

When this was brought to the attention of the Minster Provincial, by then Sister Elizabeth, by Brother Michael, her opposite number in the Society of St Francis, there appeared to be a solution. Sister Leonore had transferred to the Community of St Francis after years as an Oxford Mission Sister of the Epiphany working in Bangladesh. She spoke Bengali and was a medical doctor. Sister Leonore moved to Toynbee Hall in 1979, where she was joined by others. Her important advocacy for Muslim people in later years in Stepney will feature in the Report of the Stepney House below. Sisters and Brothers continued to work at Toynbee Hall until 1982, it is believed. Sister Elizabeth's account in 1981 reads:

> The overt presence of a Christian group wanting to live and be seen as a family within a larger community required some adjustments on both sides. Two Brothers and two Sisters are there, at first living severally in different blocks, but now occupying a flat which normally

holds six students. They have one spare room, and an all-purpose dining-cum-everything-else; the sixth room now being used as a chapel. Acceptance and integration is taking time, but they are all welcomed in their work areas, in nursing, old peoples' centre, special families' care and doctor's clinic.

Community of St Francis, 1980.

In the 1980s, when the numbers of Sisters continued to grow (numbers peaked at 55 in 1990), the number of Branch Houses also increased enormously.

1984 House Reports

The 1984 Southern Region House Reports, as well as Compton Durville, mentions the **Paddington House**, where Pauline, Jannafer and Eleanor Bridget lived:

> Pauline continues her work at the West London Day Centre, and much interest was generated, both inside and outside the Society, by her article in a recent *Troubadour*, and, subsequently, by her TV appearance on *Songs of Praise*. Homelessness and its allied problems

are becoming more and more significant in London, so any work of this kind has important implications for future ministry as well as present value.

St Mary's Hospital, W2, has had a fairly long interregnum before the appointment of a new chaplain last autumn, and Jannafer was able to assist in filling the gap. This was demanding in time and effort – and we welcomed the new chaplain – but it was valuable in forging further links in the area. Jannafer also has contacts at Paddington Station as well as in the parish.

Eleanor Bridget was able to extend her student work somewhat to include student nurses as well as medical students, and has gained some useful experience in the parish team.

Elizabeth is finding Paddington a useful base in terms of her travelling ministry.

In **Plaistow**, it is recorded:

Susan is working voluntarily as a care assistant with a group of handicapped people in a local day centre. Despite having some bouts of ill-health in the New Year she is enjoying the work very much. She is also responsible for the care of guests in the house.

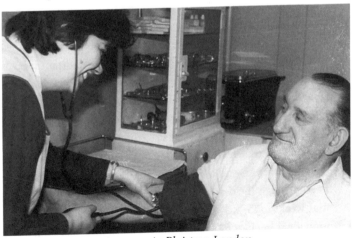

Sister Beatrice, practice nurse in Plaistow, London.

Beatrice works part-time as a District Nurse in the borough. She is also part of a group formed for cancer support locally called CYANA and has had a fairly heavy list of preaching engagements. She also gives Donald some secretarial help.

The **Stepney House**, in Halcrow Street, which included Brothers and Sisters at this time, gives a fuller sense of life in a Branch House, as well as the specifics of the ministries of each Religious (here I omit details of the Brothers).

We have been living at 10 Halcrow Street for two months short of two years and are nearly at the point where we can say that the work on the house is finished – in fact it probably never will be, but at least now all the space is usable and used.

The house is well used; we have had a lot of people to stay, personal friends, Sisters and Brothers and various others we are asked to accommodate. There have been a number of groups using the house for meetings, sometimes overnight, and guests for Offices and the Eucharist are a regular feature. People come to see individuals or all of us, often staying to lunch or supper; it's even been known for people to come for breakfast.

A good routine has been established with regular prayer times and a daily Eucharist in the house, Monday to Friday. The local clergy are very generous with their time and always seem more than willing to preside. One feature which we consider important, and seems more acceptable across the community now, is Saturday as a day free from communal obligations. That is good. It is interesting that we often spend quite a lot of it together. We have regular house 'outings' and enjoy quite a lot of each other's company.

Victor is the Guardian of the London Custody and we all benefit from his warmth and encouragement. In our house we meet weekly to go through the diary and arrange cooks, and about every three to four weeks to discuss larger and long-term issues. As there is no one individual in charge we share the responsibility, including the chair; it's hard work but does have the advantage of giving time to talking things through carefully, including the less easy, and results in a strong commitment to decisions reached together, and a strengthening of our common life. We have occasional joint visits from Anselm and Elizabeth as our Provincials when matters of joint concern are discussed. We appreciate their support and acceptance.

Each of us has a part-time paid job. They are quite different and even though we don't share a lot of the details we mostly enjoy the work we do. Probably their only common factor is that they encroach on the rest of our time as little as possible, except over lunchtime.

Leonore has continued to take the histories of Bengali patients at the Mile End Hospital and helped as interpreter at a newly started Community Health Clinic for Bengali families; linking them with health facilities and providing a preliminary examination upon arrival in Britain. She has also been used quite a lot by the Social Workers, accompanying them on visits to Bengali families in filling-in. She has worked with members of a Sidcup parish, building up links between them and a Tower Hamlets school where the children are mostly from Bengali families. This project is leading to ever widening contacts between the parishioners and the immigrant Bengali population in Stepney. Leonore has also spoken at various meetings of Tertiaries, midwives and parish groups on the difficulties Bengalis encounter living in British inner cities.

Some enthusiastic medical workers have asked to learn Bengali, including a young GP who practises nearby, and a couple of Health Visitors – one of whom has gone on to do O-level Bengali! She has been asked to advise in various areas where Bengali and English cultures are looking for common ground. Thanks to Leonore, Asian children can eat 'halal' meat for school dinners!! Leonore left Stepney on Easter Tuesday to return to Compton. She will be greatly missed, by both we who have lived with her and the many people she has befriended, supported and enjoyed in Stepney. Maureen has come to live with us. At the time of writing she has been with us a little over a week. We are glad that she has arrived …

As well as the Houses in London, Newcastle-under-Lyme became a focus for the Community of St Francis for many years.

Newcastle-under-Lyme

Clare Heath had worked in a couple of parishes in London before moving to Newcastle-under-Lyme, where she bought a large house and ran it as a residential home for elderly people. After some time she sold the house but retained the stable block, which she had converted into a house for herself with a large garden. Finding it too large, she asked a number of Anglican women's Religious Communities if they might be able to make use of the house, and eventually, in the early 1970s, she offered it to the Community of St Francis. Although the Sisters were committed elsewhere, they agreed to go and see the property, and a couple of years later began to use the house as a centre for quiet and retreat, and Clare Heath continued to live there with the Sisters. After some time the house was expanded significantly using money from a Mr and Mrs Samuels, the parents of Sister Eileen Mary, who offered to fund the project in return for making their own home there. This particular Branch House was to continue well into the 1990s.

The 1984 House Report for **Newcastle-under-Lyme** reads:

> Have you ever felt that you were under assault? Well, we have, over the last few months. A continuous stream of 'happenings' and not much time to catch our breath in between.
>
> Hilary and Noel exchanged Houses last November and we looked forward to a smooth-running House when the settling in period was over. We did think we had found the 'right mix' and were happy and relaxed in our relationships – from relaxation times to the saying of the Offices. The latter having the informality that is possible in the smaller Houses, at the same time retaining the reverence so vital to our worship. The strong relationship has made it possible for us to experience a growing openness and honesty with each other and has been a source of strength in the difficult months that have ensued.

The function of the House continues along the lines that have developed over the years of a combination of prayer and activity. We have an increasing number of individuals and groups visiting the house for rest and renewal. To date this year we have had over 400 in the House, either as daily visitors, groups, or residential guests. A significant number of these have had a need for some form of counselling or a listening ear. It is our privilege to be used in this capacity but it does take its toll, especially if we are thin on the ground for one reason or another.

The Third Order has regular meetings here as do several Parish/Diocesan Councils. There are more requests than we can accept.

We have our wayfarers still, with an average of about six a day. The numbers seem to be increasing, with quite a few new faces. We all share in providing 'tea and sympathy' – trying how best to offer friendship and a back-stop, at the same time respecting their privacy and independence.

Listening.

Eileen Mary continues to be kept busy with outside engagements – talks, Quiet Days, Retreat and a Holy Week Engagement. In addition she has undertaken a Counselling Course at Bristol, one day a month, which is almost completed. She is also a member of the Diocesan Board of Mission and Unity. In her capacity as Novice Counsellor for the Third Order there is quite an amount of time spent counselling novices or interviewing aspirants. Eileen is also helping to organize the Midland Franciscan Festival at Lichfield in June. These activities are in addition to some cooking, the shopping and the usual Guardian-type responsibilities.

Veronica is our very able laundress – of course she also gardens, a chore which she loves and does so well. She leads groups, shares in the counselling and is a happy, loving presence in the house. Unfortunately Veronica has had considerable trouble with her knee and, on medical advice, has had to devise ways of alleviating the up and down problem of the stair – not always easy.

Pat is responsible mainly for the housework and wields a wicked paintbrush to keep the House looking fresh and attractive. Recently she has spent some time in the kitchen and has discovered her hidden talents in preparing meals which have been greatly appreciated by the guests (and Sisters). Pat has some outside engagements including Missions and has the usual involvement here with guests and groups, using her counselling skills to advantage.

Noel has been in the kitchen originally, but has 'been around' since February, sharing the housework, groups and talks where possible. After a fall, she had her arm in plaster for some time, then developed back problems which have been exacerbated by the stairs. This has placed considerable strain on the House, leaving us sometimes with only two Sisters. Quite difficult if we have a large group as we are all past the first flush of youth! Nevertheless she is making her contribution to the house – with counselling and friendliness and, now that she is a lot fitter, doing what she can physically.

The present situation has emphasized the physical aspects of this House. In fact, a good balance of physical/emotional strength is desirable here because of the layout of the House and the exceptionally close proximity in which we live and work. This does create tensions and even good relationships can be tested to their limits at times.

The position of the telephone is under discussion and we are looking forward to having an alternative to having the only telephone in the house situated in Eileen's bedroom/office. This would be more convenient for all, but especially for guests.

Mr and Mrs Samuels and Miss Heath are still with us and bring their own blessings to us all.

So we go on, depending on our prayer life and trying to maintain and develop the vision of N-U-L as a house of prayer – for the larger community and for our own.

We know that, at the end of the day, God *is* in it.

In addition to guests and visitors sharing our offices – and the constant requests for intercessory prayer – we have had over 550 people sharing the Eucharist in our Chapel to date this year.

Belfast

In September 1973, the Brothers moved into two houses in the Parish of St Luke, Lower Falls, which straddled the so-called peace line between the nationalist and unionist communities. The Brothers were invited by the Bishop of Connor, Arthur Butler, in part to support Brother Kevin who had just completed his training for ordination at Trinity College, Dublin, and was to serve his title at St Luke's. The need for a praying Franciscan presence was also highly desirable for the community tensions were high at that time. Even among Anglicans in Northern Ireland, Anglican Friars were virtually unknown and the Brothers decided not to wear habits, since they would be immediately misidentified as Roman Catholics. In 1977 the Brothers moved to Deerpark Road, because their original friary was threatened with demolition. In due course they requested the presence of the community of St Francis, and two Sisters moved to live nearby.

An edited report from a Provincial meeting from 1984 reads thus:

Teresa spoke of the tension between jobs and community life and how it was possible to ignore community difficulties by becoming absorbed in work. But part-time employment supplies most of the House's running costs. It was agreed that Damian's report to the First

Order Brothers' Chapter should be read as giving a fuller picture of the situation, and that this might be circulated with the minutes.

The question of the necessity to be seen to be engaged in parish work in order to reassure the local church arose. There were particular difficulties in the Northern Ireland situation in understanding community life. How necessary was it to be closely identified with the church? It was pointed out that without the goodwill of the Bishop it would not be possible to be there at all. Service by spiritual direction and retreats would indicate a new direction for the local church.

Birmingham

In 1971, one of the Sisters went to work in Birmingham in an ecumenical hostel for girls at risk. Some had been sex workers but the majority were vulnerable for other reasons, often resulting from poverty and neglect as children; some had significant mental health issues. The programme was rehabilitative, and the young women moved on to hostels or shared flats as appropriate. The Brothers also had Houses in Birmingham, notably in Gillott Road, where, when the Brothers' work with boys on probation ceased and they moved to Frankley in 1997, the Sisters took over the House. There they remain, after a number of years when Gillott Road was the focus of care for elderly members of the Community of St Francis.

Again in 1984, this was the report:

Three Sisters at Birmingham House – Clare, Judith, Dianne.

Fortunately Deaconess Mavis White was able to help out the week Gwenfryd went, and is still helping. She is excellent with the work and appreciates the liturgical life.

We are still two members of staff short in the hostel and have advertised but the only suitable applicant had a more attractive offer of work.

We've moved from flat at 6A Edgbaston Rd to 40 Trafalgar Rd.

The hostel and staff are now complete but 40 requires external decoration be carried out in a few weeks by Copec.

It's good to be together again under the same roof yet able to get away from the girls on a day off.

We now have a chapel, the bishop has given permission for the Sacrament to be reserved and we await a Tabernacle.

Clare has completed her course and has been told she's passed but this isn't official yet.

The hostel is now functioning normally and there is more demand for places than we can meet.

Our Street

… Margaret, an Irish lady who is inclined to shout her feelings about things to the world very graphically – especially about people of darker colours and wide political issues. She has been very offensive to our Moslem neighbours, particularly to the small children. On Christmas Eve Mr Patel who lives next door came around with £5 and asked us to buy a Christmas present for Margaret. He sat and talked with Di about how sad it was for all these lonely people in the road (old), to be living on their own, as well as talking about the importance of family life and the breakdown within his own culture.

Our Sikh neighbour bought us little cakes for Divali.

In the house at the moment is a runaway Hindu girl, and her Moslem boyfriend is around a lot, with several Roman Catholics and a Pentecostal who's very lively.

At the top of the road 'Cornerstones', a Christian organization, has opened a coffee shop. It's a great asset to the community – you can sit for ages over coffee and they don't move you on. When Clare took someone in great distress in off the street the lady in charge let them have a table at the back and turned the fan extraction on to drown the crying from the other customers and contacted the local clergy to take over and transport the lady home eventually.

Jean, Veronica, Susan, Elizabeth, Beatrice all helped out over the winter months at different times and all brought their own unique contribution. Which we were grateful for.

Judith is still enjoying her studies at Westhill and assisting in a literary class.

Compton Durville

Gradually the work of the home began to dwindle, in part because of the age of some Sisters who were nurses, and the health issues of those who were younger. While some other Sisters were able to help as nursing assistants for short periods of time, there were fewer and fewer trained nurses, and the work of other Branch Houses called for some of those other skills. At the same time new regulations governing nursing homes came into force, and Compton's premises needed updating again. During the 1975 flu epidemic about half the patients died, and after this there was considerable heart-searching about this work. In due course the home ceased to be, but some Sisters took on work as community nurses among elderly people, and there was of course the care of the Community's elderly Sisters as an essential ministry.

A 1984 report reads:

Personnel

The House has had to face some major changes in the past year. The long expected death of Mother Agnes happened peacefully in July after many years of illness and infirmity and loving care by Bridget, assisted by others when needed. This freed Bridget to take over the reins of Guardian as well as to take some well-earned holiday in her beloved Scotland in July and to have three weeks rest and retreat at Turvey Abbey in November. Little did we know that shortly after this she would suffer her first heart attack, be back with us for a short while after Christmas after her stay in hospital, and suffer a second one and die so suddenly before the New Year. Her solid, wise loving and cheerful presence is still very much missed by us all.

Others have gone but not in quite the same way!

Gabriel was duly installed in her hermitage dedicated to St Mary and the Angels in August and Mary Elizabeth was admitted as a novice in the same month. Jean, who also had returned from Dover in June, went to Zimbabwe in October for three months to be with the Indigenous Community of the Holy Transfiguration and to help and encourage them as they find their way after breaking from the CZR. She expects her visa from the USA to come through any time and then will be gone from us on transfer to the American Province. Judith is still in hospital in Denbigh in North Wales and we hear from her from time to time. We are looking forward to her visiting the House for a few days at the end of May. She has had a good visit home to her family in Leeds from hospital.

Our net losses have exceeded gains and therefore there have been considerably increased demands in all work areas for the ten of us resident at the present moment. The outside call for missions and engagements does not seem to diminish; so far we have not had to cut back in what we take on in the House, but we recognize this as a possibility in the future. Some people in the house feel we need to rethink our work priorities.

Ministry

We continue to have a steady flow of individual guests and groups using our residential facilities as well as a number of individuals and groups using the conference room or other space on a daily basis. Caring for our four elderly residents continues as does the provision of meals on wheels for Shepton Beauchamp village twice a week from the home kitchen. Sr Angela is involved in regular pastoral visiting in Shepton Beauchamp and Sr Barbara visits in South Petherton.

We have gone ahead and set up the Education Project as a new ministry of the House. This has received outside funding from various trusts totalling £1,500, and encouraging support from local headteachers and RE teachers, and the first school groups are expected in June. It is hoped to get fully under way in the autumn. It is expected that novices will be involved as well as others and that it will be possible for one Sister to administer it.

General

The house timetable was changed in August and from Tuesday to Saturday we now have the Eucharist after Midday Prayer and this is proving to be workable and well received by us as well as our guests and the local priests who come so faithfully each week. On the first Sunday of each month a Sister preaches at the Eucharist and this has been good experience for us all. We value the links with Hilfield and so appreciate the Brothers who so willingly come over early each Sunday.

The Community worked for many years in the other parts of the UK, including Scotland and Northern Ireland, and its two long-standing hermits – of whom more later – made their homes in Wales.

6
2004

Day 22

But chiefest of all forms of service that the Brothers and Sisters can offer must ever be the effort to show others in his beauty and power the Christ who is the inspiration and joy of their own lives. They will seek to do this, not in a spirit of aggression, nor with contempt for the beliefs of others, but rather because, knowing in their own experience the power of Christ to save from sin and to give newness of life, they must needs seek to share their own supreme treasure. Out of the fullness, therefore, of devoted love they would seek to give their belovèd Master to all.

They must remember that, in this task of showing Christ to others the witness of life is more eloquent than that of words. Franciscans must, therefore, seek rather to be living lives through which Christ can manifest himself than to preach much in public. Nevertheless, there will be some among them called more particularly to the ministry of the Word (cf. 1 Peter 3.15), and all must be ready at all times to give an answer for the faith that is in them, and particularly to guide all who are sincerely seeking after truth. They must also be ready by instruction and prayer and spiritual direction to strengthen the faith of Christians and lead them forward in the spiritual life.

(Principles Day 22)

It is perhaps misleading and even invidious to compare numbers in the Community of St Francis in the 20 years since the last group of House reports I quoted, and the rise and fall that is detectable between 1984 and 2004 needs to be read in the light of the fact that for the first 50 years of the Community of St Francis, double figures were unknown. Nonetheless, in 1984 there appear to have been 43 Sisters rising to 55 in 1990. By 2004 there were 31. This represented a very different story from that told by Roman Catholic Apostolic Sisters, though numbers in those Roman Catholic Orders seem to have risen by 2015.

After Vatican II, numbers of Roman Catholic Sisters in northern Europe began to plummet, in part because rethinking vocation had led to disillusionment. Numbers of Sisters in southern Europe and across the global South have been maintained, however. Within an Anglican context, I believe that women's ordination first to the Diaconate, with the implied promise of priestly ordination, and then to priesthood may have had some effect on those trying their vocations as Sisters. Before ordination was a possibility, vocations to ministry might have taken the form of work as parish workers, but a Religious vocation might also have opened possibilities of a more radical ministry. Since women's ordination, my conversations at the theological college where I work suggest that at least some women who might have considered the Religious Life feel that their vocation to prayer and service can be fulfilled without the demand of Religious vows and what they see as traditional Religious Life. Pioneer ministry may also have contributed to this, enabling, as it does, ordained and sometimes lay people to minster in non-traditional contexts. I have spoken to a number of those who are interested in pioneer ministry or in neo-monasticism, who wonder whether the concept of the 'unprofessed Friar' might be useful for their ministry.

Within the Community of St Francis, the mean number of Sisters has been somewhere around 25, so the numbers in the 1980s and 1990s are anomalous. The rethinking of Religious Life among Anglicans I think in part brought that life to the forefront, in a Church that did not necessarily celebrate its Religious. The influence of Liberation Theology and its call for the preferential option for the poor also I believe influenced the response of the Community and Society of St Francis, to be more explicit about their call to be among the poor and suffering. This in at least some cases inspired women and men to seek this kind of commitment, and the work of both Society and Community sustained that inspiration. At least for some time.

In a world that is post-Christendom, and in which theologically Sisters and Brothers, nuns and monks, do not claim that theirs is a more perfect way, it is likely that Religious vocations will not be part of the 'normal' conventions of discipleship. While Elizabeth Stuart's argument that in the 1990s discipleship had 'collapsed into family life' may be rather discouraging, nonetheless family life, perhaps extended to include the church and even the 'stranger,' does seem to be an aspiration for many people, who look upon the raising of children as a key Christian calling.

Community of St Francis, 2004.

Numbers of Sisters in the Community of St Francis declined through death, some left for other communities, including the Second Order Anglican Franciscan Community at Freeland (the Community of St Clare), though others transferred to the Community of St Francis from other Anglican Societies and Sisterhoods. Some Sisters felt unable to continue in the Life. As I have hinted, some of those former Sisters I met offered reasons like the infantilization that they felt in Religious Life, others that their intellectual capacities and needs were not taken seriously. For a number it simply no longer made any sense, or 'didn't feel right anymore.' In discussing this subject Sister Elizabeth simply declared that 'they didn't have vocations'. And that is probably true, at least not in the conventional sense. I do think, however, that Sister Beverley's use of the term the Fourth Order, those who came and stayed for a time, has something in it. For some women and men, clearly vocation is temporary, or this becomes clear, and the Community of St Francis does not allow for Sisters to stay in temporary vows. Some speak of their time at the Community with great unhappiness and some resentment, but most of those with whom I have spoken express a real sense of learning something important, and tell tales of great good humour, if sometimes wryly.

The decline in the numbers of Community of St Francis Sisters towards the end of Sister Elizabeth's term as Mother and then Minister, and then for the brief time that Sister Nan was Minister and then – for longer – Sister Joyce, brought about some important changes in the Community's discernment. There was a much stronger sense at this time that the commitment of the Community of St Francis to particular places and projects needed to be reviewed regularly. At a time when many, even most, requests could not be met, the archives suggest a growing intentionality in decisions considered and reached. This is reflected in the House Reports that follow, which offer a second snapshot of the life and work of the Community of St Francis, 20 years after that of the previous chapter.

2004 House Reports

Birmingham

Past

There have been no changes in the House membership in the past year – Angela Helen, Hilary, Judith Ann and Maureen, with the hermit Sisters Gwenfryd Mary and Patricia Clare attached to us. Much of the ministry and work has continued as before. Although Angela Helen continues to be involved in a number of groups, her health has not been as good. Getting a financial contribution from Social Services towards the cost of her respite care away (see below) was a bit like trying to get water out of a stone, but we did get it in the end. During the autumn Angela has had a number of falls, and we need to take care to be around to give her help more frequently.

The end of August and the beginning of September were busy with planned work being done in the House to update the central heating system and re-lay the floor. We needed to replace part of the back garden fence which was falling down. In the middle of all of this we had 'Niagara Falls' in the kitchen when the hot water tank split one night. We were without hot water for a few days, and without most of the power circuit in the kitchen until the wiring had dried out.

Hilary: The last twelve months have continued to be well occupied. I have now completed four units of the second level of the computer studies, and plan to return this month to complete the course. The work on *Franciscan* subscriptions still takes up more time than I had anticipated originally, but I do have a clearer idea of what I am doing. Gift Aid work varies according to the time of year.

I have helped out when needed at the parish where I was previously licensed, but go less frequently, and worship at a local parish. I recently had the privilege of being the first female president at two parishes – one of which has just rescinded the Resolutions passed in 1994. I continue on the Freeland rota, and was able to fill some unexpected gaps during the year. I attend meetings of the local Residents' Association when possible.

Judith Ann: At the time of writing I'm still recovering from a shoulder blade broken some seven weeks ago. It is still painful. Some time ago I made up my mind to change churches, and looked around a little, but found that people at St A's were coming up to me and having a quiet word. Nothing very big or important, but wanting someone who had time. This is often the case at the Sunday 8.00 a.m. Often there's nothing wrong, they just want to talk about the ups and downs of their week. From this came a little visiting and I would like to do more. Often I'm asked to do the intercessions on Sunday, and I've preached a few times.

I still go to craft class. It's a good group and an interesting and interested group to be with. I still like Birmingham, and the cross-section of race and religion I meet daily – a good mix.

Maureen: This year has been busy with much the same things as last year. Lately work at the hospital has been more demanding, in part because of a Staff Nurse Development Programme I am involved with. It has introduced me to 'portfolios' (I thought they were things that politicians had) and to 'Key Skills', which is an extension of the government's obsession with test and attainment levels in things like mathematics, communication, information technology and problem solving.

I've become a bit quicker on the computer with *Franciscan* (thankfully) and continue to enjoy co-mentoring the Education for Ministry group. The correspondence course of Franciscan Spirituality from the Franciscan International Study looks as though it won't resume until September 2005.

Present

We continue to have interesting diary meetings each week as we negotiate to fit in a variety of commitments outside the house. There are weeks when we don't seem to be working together very much, but it is good that we do all have outside interests.

There is a lot of change and regeneration beginning in the neighbourhood. Early in the year the local tower block was demolished, and at the time of writing new boundary walls are being built down one side of Summerfield Crescent. When the whole of the Crescent has been dealt with then a similar plan is proposed for many of the houses at the lower end of Gillott Road. The area around Icknield Port Road is to be redeveloped with housing replacing the old industrial units, and it is hoped that the canal loop will also be re-developed and be linked in with Association but so far we don't know if the council do intend to go ahead.

Future

As always we do not know what the future holds for the House, but we look forward to whatever challenges God (or the Community) may send, praying that we may have the courage to meet them willingly and cheerfully.

The Community of St Francis - Brixton

The past year has seen little change. Catherine Joy left to set up her hermitage in Liverpool at the beginning of October and Jennifer visited us for a week in June.

We have welcomed members of CSF and SSF and family and friends to stay and have hosted some committee meetings. Members of the House have provided input for their Third Order meetings and have preached in several local churches. In Lent, we met together weekly for Lectio Divina using the Sunday Gospel readings.

The quality of community life in the House is seriously affected by Joyce's necessary absences and by Nan's chronic illness. It may prove beneficial if we seek some help in dealing with the effects of this.

A cracked window pane in the guest room has been repaired. In November, the leaking central heating boiler was changed to a slimmer model, the kitchen sink was replaced and a new worktop fitted. This was followed by redecoration of the kitchen just in time for Christmas. In spring, the old, ugly, decomposing garden shed was demolished and the next day was replaced by a bright new, considerably smaller shed which has improved the look of the garden immensely.

Joyce: As usual I have been away quite a bit during this year in the course of my responsibilities as Minister General. In July I had an added journey to Australia when my sister was in the last stages of cancer. It was a blessed time and I was glad to be with her when she died.

I am thankful that I can still live at the flat and share in the life of the House when I am here. Participating in the Mission at Southwark

Cathedral in September was a bonus in many ways. The cathedral is my parish church.

Gina: In most respects my life has continued as last year. I still work three days a week on the chaplaincy team at Wormwood Scrubs and see people at home for counselling and spiritual direction. I have completed a World Faiths Course as part of my ongoing development at the prison. This involved working on a portfolio and attending a residential at the Prison Service College.

In March my twin brother and I celebrated our 60th birthday with a big party and the next day the household here gave me a tea party followed by a meal out. A tertiary friend gave me the use of her cottage in Cornwall for a week in May as a present, so all in all I was thoroughly spoilt.

Chris(tine) James: The past year has, once again, been busy but I have continued to enjoy my activities of a two-day part-time office job and, working from home, my job as the secretary of Anglican Religious Communities and being Provincial Bursar, Computer Advisor and Vocations Advisor.

I passed my AAT Intermediate Accounting course but have decided not to continue to Technician level, which would have involved a further four terms of study for two evenings a week and lengthy project work. The Intermediate level has given me new skills to apply for the job of Provincial Bursar. I led the team of Franciscans at the Greenbelt festival and enjoyed it. The following week I attended the ARC Conference but, while it was good to be able to go, the two events so close together meant that I then had a very busy few weeks catching up and preparing for Chapter.

I am now going to an evening class on tapestry weaving, which is both (re)creative and enjoyable.

Catherine Joy: I began work as part-time Anglican chaplain at Ashworth Psychiatric Hospital in May as well as participating in the liturgical and sacramental life of Liverpool Parish Church. In August

I broke my leg in a bicycle accident and have been laid up ever since then. I expect to return to work at the end of October if cleared by my occupational therapist.

As the rector of Liverpool Parish church needs the use of the flat I have been occupying for the past year, I shall be moving to the curate's house in Walton parish, Liverpool, which is conveniently nearer to Ashworth Hospital. This move will also provide me with more seclusion and quiet with no expectations from the parish.

Compton Durville

We began the year with eight Sisters including the Minister Provincial and the Novice Guardian. We became nine when we welcomed Jennifer at the beginning of February, reverting to eight when Jackie went on leave in late September.

The main 1960s building has been completely rewired this year, and deficiencies in the fire protection rectified, and the system modernized. The guest wing, chapel and two other rooms were painted professionally as part of this process. Significant amounts of painting, and carpentry mainly to improve storage areas, have also been done by various volunteers. In Easter week a new cold-water tank was installed. Some bits of the electrical work have yet to be completed, including the loop system in the chapel and conference room, and although they are lovely people it will be a relief when the electricians have finally gone!

The hermitage needs major work, and we are delighted that the Trust is planning to replace the existing building, hopefully with a wooden prefabricated bungalow next spring. We also plan to put an extra shower in the barn guest house, and to install a disabled toilet in the main building as soon as possible.

Our self-employed gardeners, Graham and Liz, continue to do wonders on a weekly basis, as do Phyllis's 'Gardeners Practical and Prayerful' three times a year. Our link with the probation service has been successfully revived and clients on Community Punishment

Orders have built a garden path, making the orchard area accessible to wheelchair users, and are currently renewing the rockery alongside the convent building. It was a great relief to get our new office computer's glitches and the change of email address sorted early this year, and to have operational the VIP computer, which Phyllis uses constantly. We are very grateful to Jonathan especially for his help in achieving this.

We enjoyed having a sojourner from October until May, which was a huge help especially while major works were ongoing. She is currently part of a lay community. An enquirer, soon to join us as a postulant, has also spent some time living and working alongside us earlier in the year. We've has two girls doing a Duke of Edinburgh's Award project alongside us for a week, and Steve, a regular guest who works with marginalized people, has brought some of his clients for short residential working parties, which they love. We continue to receive regular help with the garden from Ann and Roger, and in chapel cleaning from Jess, as well as occasional help from other local tertiaries, and from working guests.

It was good to celebrate Liz's novicing last Francistide, and Catherine Joy's silver jubilee Eucharist and lunch late in November, managing to fit it round the major works going on at the time. In the spring we hosted the launch of two A-level Philosophy of Religion textbooks, one of which is dedicated to us here.

This springs from our ongoing link with Peter Vardy the Vice Principal of Heythrop College. We have had two House study days: one which we led ourselves on 'Colourful Prayer', and a session on Fire Procedures. We've also been able to participate in CME days at Wells free of charge, and most of us have attended at least one.

Since the beginning of 2004 we have normally been closed to guests from Sunday afternoon until Tuesday morning. This has given us more space, and made Mondays less pressured. It has felt important that we have some time with 'just us' both in the chapel, and being together in other ways. We have more recently introduced House silent days on certain Mondays.

Hospitality continues to be the major focus of our corporate ministry. A wide variety of people come, and we do a lot of related pastoral work and engagements, both here and elsewhere. Predictably the major works have had an effect on our guest statistics this year. Our number of bed nights for guests staying with us is down by around 10 per cent on last year, but an increase in self-catering guests has meant that the total number of bed nights is only down by 2 per cent at 2,202. Again unsurprisingly our day guest figures have also been affected – they are down by around 30 per cent. However, the good news is that despite lower numbers of guests and our contribution guidelines remaining static, our guest income is up. The shop income and range of stock also continues to grow significantly.

A recent development in our programme this November is an event conducted by someone from outside the community, a new departure for us. Petra Galama, a Dutch Roman Catholic research student at Bristol University, has generously offered us the gift of a weekend on Julian of Norwich, on whom she specializes. As well as 18 guests, most of the Sisters will be participating. Ray Lambie, a tertiary and former naval cook, who has cooked for our Sisters' Meetings in recent years, is happy to cook for this event, thus enabling most of the household to take part. We are most grateful. For our 2005 programme we have introduced 48-hour Prayer Workshops, one mid-week and one over a weekend, instead of the Retreats for Beginners, which we have held over the past few years. With the exception of our Centenary Open Day, the other events planned are similar to those held successfully in recent years.

Beverley: I have had a year that has been busy and challenging and stretching me in many ways. In my role as Novice Guardian I have been away quite a lot, Jennifer moved to Compton in February and she and Liz and I have attended novice units at Chigwell in term time. It remains a great privilege 'walking in the journey' with them. In September, following seven years as Guest Sister, I stepped down from that role, much to my relief. I continue to work as a volunteer with Cruse Bereavement Care in Yeovil and Sherborne area, which I value doing. I have also participated in the New Wine conference in the summer, being part of the prayer ministry team. A highlight of my year has been taking part in a women's Fun Run for Cancer Research in Somerset. I am now in training for a 10 km run, and eventually hope to do a half marathon. On a personal note, I recognize the need to stop, and be still, to prayer and let God in more. I am trying to listen!!!

Helen Julian: Most of the components of the year have remained the same – life in the House with its routines and rhythms, visiting other Houses, meetings (and more meetings!), occasional engagements, writing, aikido. Probably the most exciting event has been the publication of my second book, *The Lindisfarne Icon*, and being asked by BRF to write their Lent book for 2007. Our impending centenary takes up increasing amounts of time and energy, and the First Order Chapter and Inter Provincial Third Order Chapter, which will take place in Canterbury next year, feel as though they are looming rather. I am aware that next year sees my fiftieth birthday, and am determined to be 'fitter by fifty'; inspired by Beverley's example I've begun some very gentle running and am extremely surprised to be enjoying it.

Jackie: This has not been the easiest of years because of various health issues, but I have made an excellent recovery ... however, I am feeling isolated and separated from the community ... I have ... decided to take a year's leave of absence, to stand back, pray, think, assess, and to decide my future. I very much enjoyed the families camp this year but am adamant that it was my last one. Have continued as a school governor at the local junior school. I have continued to speak to various meetings and schools. Enjoy preaching, leading quiet days and retreats. I have done a fair bit of pastoral work and one-to-one counselling.

Jannafer: Another year gone already – but at least now I do have a bus pass! Life is very much the same for me as last year in terms of work within the House. My foot is much better, for which I am most grateful. My Mum's sister, Auntie Peggy, was found dead on the floor at the end of April, which was a shock. As expected, I was executor of her will – times away from here were needed and generously given.

Jennie: Another much enjoyed year at Compton. Never a dull moment. I have taken a Retreat for Beginners again this year and this time they were absolute beginners. I found it a great privilege and joy to share that time with them. I have also led two or three Quiet Days, taken a couple of services at a residential home in Yeovil. I attended the Justice conference in London in May and in September the AGM also in London. Also with my JPIC hat on I continue to attend the South Somerset Peace Group, which meets monthly in Illminster.

Jennifer: I thank every member in this province for welcoming me warmly and appreciate the opportunity to attend novice units/conferences and other related events/experiences as well as the short visits to Houses away from Compton. It seems right to be here for my final novitiate and I am glad to be here. I suppose I would describe that sense of satisfaction like arriving at the centre of a labyrinth walk, laying down 'stories' which I heard, some partially spoken, some unspoken and some incomplete, and being drawn personally into some of these stories, which in turn demand my prayers, reflections and challenging responses with the possibilities of death-dealing or life-engendering choices.

Liz: A year since my novicing and I'm still here!! I don't know where the time has gone! It has certainly been an eventful year on a personal level, with some difficult things to work through. But this has been made possible by the prayers, patience, support and love of my Sisters, who have all been there for me in their different ways – thank you. This year I led my first Parish Group for a Quiet Day, led a meditation for the MU in South Petherton on Maundy Thursday, went to Greenbelt, presided regularly at the Eucharist and generally contributed to the cooking and cleaning within the House. I have also continued to work on the computers to try to iron out some of the glitches and keep them running smoothly, including the Sisters in their computer endeavours. I have also developed my interest in photography with the aid of a digital camera and have enjoyed snapping away and making cards to sell in the Compton shop and the odd photo for the *Franciscan*.

Phyllis: This past year seems to have been more of the same – spiritual direction, House Bursar, garden, Churches Together in South Petherton, PCC, Deanery Secretary and visiting Burnworthy Rest Home, yet with a more positive and less tense feel to it. I believe this is partly due to the IGR I had at Loyola Hall just before Christmas, when my guide said at our first session, 'Do nothing!' having sensed my task-centredness . It was really difficult yet extremely valuable not only for myself but also for some of the people I have seen either for spiritual direction or to guide them in their IGRs. A newer deepened experience of being.

Three more Gardeners Prayerful and Practical retreats have been held and these are fruitful both spiritually and 'horticulturally'. I enjoy my liaison work with those who come on Community Punishment Orders – and their efforts are mentioned elsewhere. One client who has just completed his Order said how much he had valued working here and being appreciated.

The VIP counter has been a great help since its installation in February, and I am grateful for the support and understanding I receive as I try to live with the frustration of deteriorating sight.

Sue: This year the building maintenance aspect of my role as Guardian has inevitably been a major preoccupation. This is not something I enjoy, so I have been especially grateful for the spiritual direction, retreat work and a variety of engagements at Compton and elsewhere, which I find fulfilling and energizing. In addition it has recently become necessary for me to take on the role as Guest Sister, which I share with Jennie. Having been a Guest Sister here for some years previously, I am very familiar with the work, which I enjoy. However, combining it with being Guardian is a new challenge. I also continue to co-ordinate the South West Spiritual Directors Network, and to be part of the leadership team for the diocesan Exploring Spirituality course.

I value my times at Freeland as chaplain, and my regular visits to Glasshampton for space and quiet. I have also enjoyed a wonderful holiday at Alnmouth and on Holy Island courtesy of the Brothers.

I am very grateful for the support and encouragement I receive from various quarters, and particularly for the cheerful co-operation of my Sisters here.

Newcastle Under Lyme

In 2002 the House closed, and Teresa was living on her own at a different address, until 2006, when she moved to Birmingham.

Teresa: This year seems to have passed with amazing speed. I have again been very busy in the parish, and I realize just how much I enjoy visiting people, whether at home or in hospital, or just chatting to people in the street.

I continue to go up to Scotland every two months or so. My Brother is declining very noticeably, and my sister-in-law Barbara is quite wonderful but going through an agonizing time. I keep in close touch with her on the phone. I still see a number of people for spiritual direction and counselling, and this keeps me out of mischief (mostly!).

I have been visited by five Sisters this year. Thank you all, it has been wonderful.

Stepney

The past year has been similar to the year before, with the same Brother to Sister balance, and this has worked very well on the whole. However, Kentigern John left for New Zealand on 6 October, so we are now getting used to our smaller number. Being one of the few

London Houses, we host various First and Third Order meetings as well as making our guest rooms available to a variety of people. Long may we continue in our ministry of hospitality!

With our reduction in numbers and due to Chris and Jason's Wednesday commitments, we have decided to cancel our 'open-house' on a Wednesday evening for the time being and look at other ways of sharing our hospitality – we intend to invite our one *regular* Wednesday visitor, and any others, to supper on other evenings. We now meet for the Eucharist after Morning Prayers on Wednesdays. On Mondays we are usually joined by three others for Monday Prayers and occasionally a friend joins us for Evening Prayer during the week. We are grateful to a local Third Order priest, as well as others, who stand in as President when Elizabeth is away.

Chris: My life continues very much as it has over the past few years with involvement in preaching, mission and Holy Week. My job with Deafblind UK continues to provide variety and challenge, particularly with my Stage 2 British Sign Language exam coming up in December.

My greatest source of interest at the moment is a Windows 98 computer, which I never thought would grab my attention in the way it has! Kentigern gallantly provided a crash-course before he left, and Jason has the noble task of continuing my education.

My thanks to Elizabeth for her cheerful support.

Elizabeth: I suppose getting older (or should it be old?!) makes life necessarily slower and so it feels more busy! I've collected a few more people for spiritual direction, and still go round to others; there have been quite a number of 'fillings-in' for the deanery and invitations elsewhere. Sadly, I had to let down one local parish for four consecutive Sundays in the Spring, being deaf from a virus and ear infection. However, all's well again on that front.

I have enjoyed compiling the 'Book of Life' – departed Sisters – and 'Memories' for CSF centenary, though there was some work involved. I can't begin to be more than a novice on the computer, so production of these has gone to the expert – Chris James – and we look forward to the finished booklets.

One of the 'jobs' I have acquired is the supply of quotations for Church Diaries (which Tristram did) and I find that quite interesting and thought-provoking. However, the possibilities are limited. Last year I sent in three short totally innocuous quotes from the Qur'an – and these were rejected by a section of the recipients.

Dundee Mid Craigie

Past

1   Genesis 12.1: The Lord said to Abraham, 'Leave your country, your family and your father's house, for the land I will show you.'

2   Moyra was returning home, after a long time away. I came as a stranger. The stranger has a unique vocation to receive. It is a mistake to want to give, to make a mark, too quickly. You have first to show respect to your hosts. To learn the history, the accent, the culture, the pronunciations of the place names, let alone the bus routes and the church politics. All is new to the stranger, who comes in need of the host's generosity. We have spent a lot of time explaining ourselves, why we have come, and what is the Franciscan way. In turn we have asked a lot of questions, wanting to understand. Thirty six times the Bible commands, 'love the stranger in your midst'. Only one verse commands love your neighbour as yourself.

3   It is now almost a year since we moved Houses. The difference between here and Barrowfield is not small but there are similarities, and to some extent life carries on as normal. There is the same round of prayer, with two or three gathered together in a small chapel, surrounded by the community of people whose troubles and joys we are here to hold up to God. Out of the chapel window we can see the two churches 100 yards away, St Ninian's Scottish Episcopal Church and Mid-Craigie Parish

Church (Church of Scotland). We join with their two small congregations to witness to the gospel by what we do in Mid Craigie.

Present

It is not as rough here as Barrowfield. There is less litter and graffiti; fewer burnt out cars and sofas. The council housing is interspersed with substantial areas of new bought houses, with neat gardens and cars being washed on Saturday morning. The area has come a long way in the last ten years. Yet all the same issues are here to be grappled with. It remains within the Social Inclusion Partnership, an area highest on the scale to measure poverty, with special funds for its regeneration.

Moyra: The main, overriding theme of this year has been the move to Dundee; and settling in.

After the long wait, we eventually moved in on 1 December 2003 … and spent the next few weeks decorating and dealing with various workmen of one variety or another. I saw far too much of Transco in the first ten days here, and we were mutually delighted when the difficulty with Scottish Hydro Electric Gas was resolved, and my working meter card was in my possession (which it should have been from the day we moved in).

While I've been looking around for some part-time, paid employment, I've also been slowly, but carefully getting to know the area. I've been on the management committee of the local, annual festival, which was a mixed blessing. I've begun working with the local Girls' Brigade on a regular basis, which I'm enjoying. It now means it's virtually impossible for me to set foot outside the house without meeting at least one child I know. The Midlin (Mid Craigie/ Linlathen) Day Care Project for the Elderly meets daily in MidCraigie Church of Scotland church, which is just across the road from our flats. While I don't volunteer there on any regular basis, I do take the mid-week service there once a month or so, and often stay on for the

afternoon activities. We also get invited to all their special events –
and it's a good place to meet people.

One of the biggest changes in life here, as opposed to life in
Barrowfield, is our relationship with the local church. The local
Episcopal church is literally on the doorstep – step foot outside
number 16, and there is St Ninian's , nothing like the 20-minute walk
or bus ride involved in getting to church on a Sunday in Barrowfield.
I've not yet been to a local meeting where church members have not
been a significant, active part of the work. It's very much a community
church, and this is reflected by the very high involvement of its
members in local community activities. I enjoy playing my clarinet
or the piano, whichever is asked of me, for services.

Engagements away from Dundee are minimal – though I did go
to the International Chapter of the Pilgrims of St Francis, which they
had requested I did, if possible, when I asked to stop being the official
Link person.

On the C/SSF front, I was part of the planning for the Sisters'
meeting in February, and have to admit to being responsible for
the creation of the large floor jigsaw that was featured in the May
Franciscan – which also produced, for me, the most positive and
memorable session of any Sisters' meeting I have ever been to. I'm
part of the Liturgy group for the CSF Centenary. I'm also House
Bursar, and responsible for producing the accounts for the Minister
Provincial SSF. Being the Webster for the C/SSF website has proved
an interesting challenge and an increase in the amount of spam email
I get.

Since moving away from Barrowfield, we have maintained contact
with several people in the area, who had been an important part of
our lives there – mainly by phone and we have visited occasionally.

7

At Home – Many Ministries

Day 3

The community, recognising that God has at all times called certain of his children to embrace a state of celibacy for the kingdom of heaven's sake, that they may be free to give themselves without distraction to his service, sets before itself the aim of building up a body of men and women who shall be completely dedicated to him alone both in body and spirit. These, after a sufficient period of probation, voluntarily in response to God's call, dedicate themselves to a life of devotion to our Lord under the conditions of poverty, chastity and obedience.

Day 4

It is not without reason that these three conditions have ever been embraced by those desiring to live the life of religious detachment; for they stand for the ideal of perfect renunciation of the world, the flesh and the devil, which are the three great enemies of the spiritual life.

(Principles Days 3 and 4)

Hermits

The Sisters of the Community of St Francis, as I have indicated, regarded themselves as a 'mixed' community, both apostolic and contemplative. From time to time Sisters transferred from the Community of St Francis to the Community of St Clare in Freeland, and thus to an enclosed contemplative life. There was some traffic in the opposite direction too. The Franciscan tradition had such a strong commitment to prayer, however, that some Sisters received permission to have more prayer time while leading apostolic lives. St Francis' own life reflects that of the Gospel accounts of Jesus, who withdrew on a regular basis, and the Hermitary website article on St Francis argues that he was drawn to the *carceri* – little cells within hermitages that were common at that time in Italy. St Francis seems to have provided for periods of prayer, particularly following strenuous apostolic work, and, although popularly understood as the most apostolic of saints, he did consider embracing a life of solitude and prayer, and this was such a strong tug that he felt compelled to consult both St Clare and one of the earliest Brothers – to help him discern God's calling. They both affirmed him in a prayerful mendicant life.

Also quoted on the *Hermitary* website, Thomas Celano's *Legenda Maior* relates a long monologue of Francis' dilemma:

> In prayer [i.e. solitude] we purify our sentiments and unite them with the one, true, supreme God and give new strength to virtue; in preaching, however, the spirit becomes sullied and drawn in many directions and loses some discipline … However, there is one thing in preaching's favour, and it seems that in God's eyes it outweighs everything else, and that is that for the salivation of souls, God's only-begotten Son, infinite Wisdom left the Father's bosom and renewed the world with his example, speaking to people the Word of salvation.[6]

Here the imitation of Christ seems to be paramount, so the *pattern* of preaching and healing and withdrawal was perhaps most important.

Part of St Francis' care for the Brothers, and for himself, was, however, the provision of a Rule for Hermits, and this has been revived in both the Community and the Society of St Francis, to allow for solitaries within the communities. It seems likely that Francis wrote the Rule for Hermits as a Rule for temporary withdrawal, following the eremitical hermits of the East. Thus Donald Spoto (also quoted in *Hermitary*) describes a tradition of eremitical life from the East that was not at all in contradiction to St Francis' mendicant calling:

> Hermits lived alone, following the customs of the Byzantine tradition, which included solitude, silence, fasting on bread and water, prayer

---

6 www.hermitary.com/articles/francishtml.

vigils and, to avoid idleness, craft work ... But their desire for solitude did not mean they turned their backs on the world completely, for they were much involved in trying to alleviate society's problems, serving as wandering preachers, aiding visitors, helping weary travelers and generally assisting the needed. (Spoto, 2003, p. 62)

The Rule for Hermits is fascinating in that it provides for Guardians of the hermit, which Francis calls 'mothers and sons'. He provides for groups to share in the life of the hermit, under the guidance, protection and sometimes provision of the mothers. But there is no sense of a spiritual elite in this Rule – for the hermits and the mothers are to swap roles, enabling each to withdraw.

Hermits are often called solitaries in the twentieth century and beyond, in part because the word 'hermit' frequently carries a sense of an unkempt man with long hair and a beard, living in a cave. The term 'solitary' does not, however, do justice to Francis' ideal. Both the Society and the Community of St Francis have nonetheless had hermits who followed an eremitical life for long period of time, but usually associated with a monastic House or friary. It should be noted, however, that the Society of St Francis at Burghwallis is the only example of the Rule for hermits being lived out; all other hermits have been solitaries, though the Metheringham House tries to follow elements of the Rule for Hermits one day each week. The most famous of the Society of St Francis' hermits was probably Brother Ramon, author of many books on Franciscan spirituality, who lived alone, testing his vocation from a caravan in the grounds of the Society of the Sacred Cross in Tymawr, and later living in the grounds of Glasshampton Monastery.

If not many are hermits, the call to solitude is significant among Anglican Franciscans, and in an unattributed paper, possibly by Sister Elizabeth, from the Community of St Francis' Chapter in June 1997, A. M. Allchin (Allchin, 1977) is quoted:

'It [the life of a solitary] is not a way to be undertaken unadvisedly, lightly, or wantonly, and it will not ordinarily be undertaken without some considerable experience of a regular life of prayer and obedience lived in community'; while a recent writer in *Signum* says, 'cenobitics are scathing about the "lucky ones" who can opt out of the hard reality of Christian living … If there are such, the life itself soon finds them out.'

The anonymous writer goes on:

> Prayer is at the heart of life for us all, but for the hermit there is the call to give it the priority of time and effort. It is a call to live a disciplined routine, night and day, balanced by manual work and by sufficient maturity and intellectual resource to support this concentration of energies.

As this writer notes, being a hermit has not much to do with introversion, for at least one of the Community of St Francis hermits was 'gregarious'.

The 1997 document gives a report of the three hermits within the Community of St Francis, and Helen Julian also has joined this number. All three had been members of the Community of St Francis for a number of years. The Compton Cricket Pavilion, given by the owner of the Manor House and adapted, was used by Sisters and retreatants until the closure of Compton Durville. Sister Gabriel moved there in 1983, 20 years after her profession. Later, in 1997, she moved to the Birmingham House and died in 1999. Sister Gwenfryd Mary moved to a bungalow at Milford Haven found for her by the Church in Wales in 1990, 23 years after her profession. The final hermit was Sister Patricia Clare, who, as well as her relationship with the Community of St Francis, had tested her vocation at the Community of St Clare, Freeland, and as a Third Order Solitary. She was professed, however, in the Community of St Francis in 1984, and in 1995 moved to a cottage in Wales bought by her family. Sister Catherine Joy lived as an urban solitary in Liverpool from 2003 until 2008, while working at the secure psychiatric hospital.

The 1997 document notes that the three Sisters continued to receive good spiritual direction, but all three Sisters 'have come through considerable nervous strain', though whether this is linked with their solitary lives is not made clear. Given that one in four women in Britain receive some form of medication for mental health issues in the course of their lives, this seems not especially alarming. One of the Sisters, because of blindness, had to receive much more support than the others, and as old age has affected them, again support has changed appropriately.

The 1997 document gives a brief account of Sister Gwenfryd Mary's life:

> Gwenfryd's spirituality is Celtic and creation centred, but supported by considerable reading. She writes and pursues her art, grows her own vegetables and acts as caretaker of the chapel of St Thomas in the garden. Pilgrims come but she sees little of them, being occasionally asked for information. She does her own shopping, as do most modern hermits; and attends her parish church (just round the corner) for regular communion. She does not have the Sacrament reserved as the other two do.

The Community of St Francis hermits were always at least nominally attached to one of the other Houses, and were regularly visited by the Minster Provincial. In 2004, Sister Gwenfryd Mary and Sister Patricia Clare make their year's reports via the Birmingham House:

> *Gwenfryd Mary:* On looking back at the last 12 months I am glad to say that it has been a good year for me. With my regained energy and health I have been able to tackle some of the gardening jobs around here! Still a lot more to do, but I feel that I now have more strength and health with which to approach them. Long may it last!
>
> I continue to do art work and have got used to the technical adjustments which I made a few years ago in order to accommodate my sight problems. These work very well. During the summer I had my usual two exhibitions at the gallery in Haverford West, and also took part in a group show. I'll never make a fortune out of it, but at least I can make some 'pin-money'! This goes towards the costs of materials to keep it all going.
>
> The number of visitors to the little chapel was fewer during this summer. Probably partly due to the heavy amounts of rain which

we had during the holiday season The weekly Eucharist continues on a regular basis, with some support from three or four of the parishioners. The curate has left the parish …

My daily round of prayer and meditation continues quietly and steadily. I am greatly blessed and privileged to be living here.

My gratitude to you all for enabling and supporting me. With my thoughts, prayers and love.

Patricia Clare: This year has been especially busy with guests coming and going from the house, but by the end of this month (October) things will be more slack. It has been a struggle to retain a sense of 'solitude', and I plan to have a less crammed diary next year. There are lots of jobs waiting to be done, and having Laurie Boorman here at the beginning of November will be a tremendous help.

Mostly people come now for a retreat, and this makes a difference to the feel of things, but it has been good to have Sue and her sister here on holiday late in October, and Gwrnfryd and her dog Mollie at the beginning of the month.

I continue to be grateful for the prayers from and link with the Birmingham House, and for visits from Elizabeth and Helen Julian. Ted and Helen Thomas still come once a month for a Eucharist, which is held in the hermitage when the house is let, but in the house otherwise.

All callings in the Religious Life are particular, and women's Religious Communities, like men's, have grown better I believe at working with individuals called to share a common life. Sister Helen Julian's life in recent years has been a good example of that. While Minister Provincial, Sister Helen Julian felt a call to a life of greater solitude, not it should be noted to the life of a hermit. She was given permission to explore that life, holding it together with continuing to be Minister Provincial which calls upon a good deal of travel and talking with individuals and in committees in order to guide the Community. While this exploration was taking place, Sister Helen Julian's call to priesthood re-emerged, and after some delay as she and the Community continued to see where

God was leading in relation to a solitary life, she was given permission to explore ordination. Sister Helen Julian was accepted for training and, while living as a solitary at Freeland, the home of the Community of St Clare, trained at Ripon College, Cuddesdon, and commenced 'serving her title' as a curate in Oxford Diocese, something completed in Southwell and Nottingham Diocese. During this period, Sister Sue was elected to be Minister Provincial, and Sister Helen Julian elected to be Minister General. Coming as her vocation to priesthood did at a time when pioneer ministry was beginning to find a high profile in the Church, perhaps Sister Helen Julian's particular combination of gifts, skills and callings was understood as part of that pioneering ethos by the Church. Whatever the case, her life, like that of all her Sisters, and indeed all people, is a work in progress and a place where God's presence and will is made known.

Priests

The response to the ordination of women as priests in the Church of England in 1994 differed from Anglican Religious Community to Religious Community. It should also be noted that at least unofficially a number of Roman Catholic Orders, and individual Roman Catholic nuns and Sisters, were very supportive of this development. Within the Community of St Francis there were a number of supporters and active members of the Movement for the Ordination of Women, most prominently, perhaps, Sisters Joyce and Hannah, and at one time Sister Hannah's television appearances brought her fairly regularly into the public gaze. Sister Helen Julian took part in the Waiting Witness outside the General Synod on several occasions, and was, with others, present outside General Synod when the Women Priests Measure was passed. Later in this chapter I will mention the pioneering work in which Sisters Hannah and Joyce were engaged, not least with regard to inclusive and what was then called 'experimental' liturgy. What is important here is to note that, as the early Fathers and Mothers of the Church recognized, *lex orandi, lex credendi* is a watchword for how theology, which is always practical, develops. By enabling and producing liturgy that embodied and asserted the authority of women, those who gathered to pray and write together as members of the Movement for the Ordination of Women were contributing to a change of climate into which the new legitimacy of women priests in 1994 might begin to flourish.

St Francis, unlike many of those who founded the great Religious Orders, was not a priest. He was persuaded to become a Deacon, though his identity as *il poverello* may have balked even at this. Throughout the history of monasticism, and the development of the mendicant orders, however, priesthood has been a significant calling alongside that of the Religious Life. On a purely pragmatic level, for those who worked in missions where priests were few, it was simply a part of servant ministry to be able to preside at the sacraments, especially at the Eucharist. Because the ordination of men in Religious Life was so common, not much reflection upon this dual vocation has been done, and discussions on the relationships between lay and ordained Brothers have tended to focus on issues of status and authority and how these affect that relationship.

Vocations to priesthood have become an important part of the life of the Community of St Francis, and two of the Sisters currently professed were ordained before they joined the community, one as an Anglican priest, the other initially a Methodist then Anglican Deaconness and Deacon and ordained priest the year before she joined the Community of St Francis. One other Sister, now ordained, speaks of a vision she received, aged 16, of herself as missionary, Sister and priest long before women's ordination was a likelihood. Of those who sought ordination while already professed, it was perhaps helpful that the first was Sister Elizabeth, who had led the community for so many years. Her ordination was shortly followed by Hilary's, another senior member of the community. It should be noted that not all the Sisters who sought ordination were selected. Quite how supportive individual Sisters were of women's ordination to Anglican priesthood is not known, but from the 1980s I am told that 'it was not an issue', unlike in the Society of St Francis where women's ordination caused some deep divisions. A perhaps unique, and it seems very prophetic and Franciscan aspect of the Community's approach, was that leadership and ordination were neither necessarily nor inevitability linked. While ordination was respected as an extension and expression of an existing vocation for those who were believed to be called to it, priesthood really did not carry with it additional status or authority. Helen Julian's election as Minister Provincial in 2002 while still lay is a very good example of this.

There was a strong sense from the early days of women's ordination that there needed to be some congruence between a vocation to Religious Life and to priesthood, and that these were not separate vocations. Unlike the Society of St Francis, which has run some parishes for many years, like St Botolph's in Cambridge, St Matthew's in Doncaster and St Matthias', Canning Town, it has never been the intention of the Community of St Francis to take on the running of parishes, though curacies have to be served, and some Sisters are assistants in parishes from time to time, and clearly flourish in that setting. At present, every House of the Community of St Francis has a resident priest from among the Sisters. The discernment process is inevitably twofold, first from within the community itself, where sometimes Sisters have been asked to delay in order that other commitments might be fulfilled. After some experimentation it was decided that the Church's discernment process should be negotiated through the sponsorship, as it were, of the Bishop Protector. This has greatly facilitated the process, because at least some grasp of what ordination for Religious might look like can been relied upon, and indeed more than a basic understanding of Religious Life can be assumed. The focus of vocation has tended to be sacramental, for some highly sacramental, at least in part because many of the functions that Deacons and priests fulfil are already a regular part of the ministry of Sisters, including for some, for example, preaching, pastoral care, involvement in development projects for the wider community, and specific ministries among disabled people. Eucharist and blessing seem to be at the heart of these Sisters' priestly vocations. As Sister Helen Julian put it: 'Hands seem very important, holding up the world to God, recognizing and celebrating the presence of God in the ordinary.' Again there is a recognition that all the Sisters – to use my words, not theirs – participate in priesthood in some way, and that the priestly calling is a particular not a better way. In the community of St Francis, priests, as I have indicated already, do not have privileges as part of a priestly hierarchy, and Sister Hilary, for example, very much wants to reject a model of priesthood that promotes hierarchy and the idea that 'Father knows best', something she believes she holds in common with her Sisters. Hilary was also very clear that it had not been her task, though she respected those who felt they should do this, to campaign or lobby for women's ordination. She tells with relish the story of one of her slightly reluctant Sisters saying of her [Sister Hilary's] presiding, 'that wasn't a woman, that was a priest', a very different stance from that taken by others. It may be that this is the spirit that makes her say that as a presider, 'I am there to enable something to happen, and my personality doesn't matter.'

Sister Liz began exploring her vocation to Religious Life when still a curate, and recognized later what a 'big thing' it was to give up the opportunity to be vicar, though she is conscious that she had always felt called to be both a priest and part of a praying community: 'So that the community is the rootedness in prayer and then from that base going out and doing your ministry in the parish.' Giving up the parish aspect of this calling had been enormously costly for the seven years or so she spent in it:

> But God knows better than I do. [Now] I can't separate the two ... somehow my priestly ministry embodies who I am ... and ... in terms of the Franciscans, it feel it is incarnational, I am expressing my Franciscan vocation in an incarnational way by going out and ebbing among the people within the parishes ... Somehow this is different from how it was before [I came into Community] ... this is more the real me ... Even when I preside – very very powerfully I feel God, the presence of God, and that is very very different from when I was just in the parish ... It feels more prayed ... as though the Spirit takes over.

Words from the Sister priests echo those of Sisters talking of vocation more generally. For Sister Sue, now Minister Provincial, and whose life embraced Methodism, including being a Methodist Deaconess, there is a sense of homecoming, and a real affirmation of Franciscan joy in a life integrated:

> In my years as an Anglican priest and Franciscan Sister there has been a deep sense of homecoming. However within that experience I have come to recognize more clearly treasures of the Methodist heritage which were so significant in my earlier Christian formation, and which continue to nourish me. When God called me into CSF I knew almost nothing about the Franciscan tradition. Yet as a postulant and novice I kept discovering Franciscan emphases that seemed to express what had been important to me all my life, much of it springing, I believe, from the Methodist ethos I had absorbed from childhood. There is a holistic approach to faith which naturally encompasses justice issues, a real sense of belonging to the Church world-wide, joyful response to God's radical generosity, passion and compassion tempering each other, and a lively expectation of finding Christ in actual human experience, in all of life, the ordinary, the appalling, and the wonderful.

Charismatics

It should be noted, as I begin this section, that though the Community of St Francis had its origins within Anglo-Catholicism, it is now a much more broad Community, and while liturgy is of high importance, the Community of St Francis does not assume that only one kind of liturgy is an acceptable and appropriate offering to God. Likewise, its theology is diverse, embracing the Catholic, evangelical and liberal, and for the most part being suspicious of labels.

Charismatic revival in the Church of England is often associated with evangelicalism, but just as this phenomenon has been highly influential in the Roman Catholic Church following Vatican II, so has it been within the part of the Anglican Church that identifies itself as Catholic. This is hardly surprising, since the Catholic tradition, as well as the Protestant and Reformed, has long taken holiness seriously, and within the Catholic West, the mystical and ineffable has been a key feature of theology and spirituality. Although the great mystics have regarded faithfulness in prayer as far more important than 'spiritual experiences', such experiences were regarded as if not 'ordinary', then at least an anticipated part of the range of God's action in the world through God's Church and individuals. Looking at the website for the On Fire Mission, one of the key agencies, in this case associated with Anglican Catholicism, I am not surprised to see a picture of a Sister of the Community of St Francis, clutching a prayer flag. The influence of charismatic Christianity has been significant for a number of the Community of St Francis Sisters, and has been an important resource for sustaining the Religious Life over many years, a number of Sisters speaking of the healing they have received through charismatic ministry.

On Fire expresses its purpose as:

On Fire Mission is a network, rooted in the Church of England but open to all, which is dedicated to promoting Charismatic renewal blended with the riches of Catholic spirituality.

At the heart of our work is an annual conference serving as a resource to clergy and laity alike. This provides an opportunity to experience personal renewal through lively sacramental worship, Bible study and retreat time, network with like-minded individuals and becoming part of a prayerful community seeking to support and minister to one another.

One Sister, influenced more broadly by the charismatic movement as well as being associated with On Fire, regularly attends New Wine conferences, where she can be found as a participant and also a member of prayer teams. Franciscans are also highly visible at the very different Greenbelt festival. Although sometimes regarded with scepticism by other Sisters, there is something very striking about the way an intense and charismatic focus on prayer can resource a life that is tough, down-to-earth and frequently challenging. There are other forms of such prayer, as exacting and supportive, as surprising and incomprehensible, but perhaps this gift of prayer makes especial sense of the Franciscan focus on joy and the extravagant love of God. The third 'Note' of the Order, *joy*, is expressed thus in the *Principles*:

Sister Liz presiding at Greenbelt.

Day 28

Finally, the Brothers and Sisters, *rejoicing in the Lord always* (Philippians 4.4), must show forth in their lives the grace and beauty of divine joy. They must remember that they follow the Son of Man, who *came eating and drinking* (Luke 7.34), who loved the birds and the flowers, who blessed little children (cf. Mark 10.16), who was *a friend of tax collectors and sinners* (Matthew 11.19), who sat at tables alike of the rich and the poor. They will, therefore, put aside all gloom and moroseness, all undue aloofness from the common interests of people and delight in laughter and good fellowship. They will rejoice in God's world and all its beauty and its living creatures, *calling (nothing) profane or unclean.* (Acts 10.28)

They will mingle freely with all kinds of people, seeking to banish sorrow and to bring good cheer into other lives. They will carry with them an inner secret of happiness and peace which all will feel, if they may not know its source.

(Principles Day 28)

132

Liturgy and Power

The Community of St Francis has made two major contributions to the liturgical life both of the Church of England and more broadly. The first contribution was shared with the Society of St Francis in the development of an appropriate Daily Office Book, and its revision. Second, the development of feminist and inclusive liturgies, both in facilitating, writing and publishing, was brought much more into the mainstream of the churches. Sister Joyce played a significant part in both these contributions, and former Sister Hannah mainly in relation to the latter.

Most of the Anglican Religious Communities, male and female, that were founded in the nineteenth and early twentieth centuries, including the Community of St Francis, began by using some version of a Benedictine Daily Office. Often long and quite complicated to work one's way around, this was found not to be particularly helpful for Apostolic Orders, for whom the regularity of the Hours were almost impossible to keep when working, for example, as nurses or even as parish workers. Gradually, the Office Book was tailored to different circumstances, and generally a simplification began to take place. I have already mentioned the decision by the community of St Francis to use Morning and Evening Prayer from the Book of Common Prayer because this made the lives of Sisters on parish mission very much easier, joining in, as it were, with the prayer of the whole Anglican Church. At the same time some of the night-time offices were halted, or retimed. These developments were not intended to suggest that every Hour was not a time for turning to God, but rather made a stronger assertion that all of life might be turned Godwards, and consequently all of life is, or can be, prayer. Sister Beverley, when she speaks to ordinands and student ministers about Franciscan spirituality, often talks about it being spirituality 'on the hoof', but what strikes me more about the prayer, not least at the Leicester House, is that it really is offering every moment to God. In the intercessions that are part of each Office, the people encountered, the work attempted, the wider life of city and world and church are prayed for in a spirit of thanksgiving or lament, of concern or plea. There is a very real sense, in sharing these prayers, of a life that is prayer.

The publication of the *Alternative Service Book* of the Church of England, authorized for public worship alongside the Book of Common Prayer, had a mixed reception. While on the whole the use of modern language was commended there was a sense that, as Petà Dunstan writes: 'the new ASB Offices were considered to be "thin"' (Dunstan, 1997, p. 311), so Brothers Tristam and Colin Wilfred SSF, and Sister Joyce CSF, worked astonishingly quickly to produce the new Daily Office SSF, published in 1981. Much to everyone's surprise the new Office Book was not only well received, but was sold out within the year, and in 1985 it was reprinted. Petà Dunstan uses the term 'ASB Office enriched' (p. 312), and then comments regarding the Society of St Francis decision to use the ASB Psalter, suggesting 'an enrichment of what had been approved by the General Synod' (p. 312). It was during this period that the Daily Office SSF came to be used as an almost standard Office Book in many Anglican Churches. By the time a further reprint was necessary, including a major revision, which had been piloted at Broxton, it was proposed that the 1992 Daily Office SSF should be published in two versions, one for Franciscans with a special supplement, and one for general use, which would be called *Celebrating Common Prayer*. Pre-publication orders sold out before the 1992 launch of *Celebrating Common Prayer*, and as Petà Dunstan again notes, 40,000 copies had been sold. Despite being called in one theological college, 'Celebrating Complicated Prayer', the popularity and ubiquity of *CCP* was such that when *Common Worship* was first mooted, some suggested that the Church of England simply adopt *CCP*. In the end this did not happen, though *Common Worship: Daily Prayer* is very obviously and extensively modelled on *CCP*. There were significant differences, however, between the Psalter of Daily Office SSF and that of *Common Worship*, and so when the Daily Office SSF was reprinted in 2010 it was decided to bring the Psalter into line with that in *Common Worship*: the Community and Society again trying to make links between their own practice and 'ordinary' Christian discipleship.

The extraordinary approbation with which the Daily Office in its various forms was met surely raised the profile of both Community and Society, and despite the general unfamiliarity with Religious Life in much of the Church of England, there was for a time a considerably greater recognition of Franciscans as the originators of these important resources.

The other theological and liturgical movement with which the Community of St Francis has been closely associated is that of Christian feminism. Both feminists, Sisters Joyce and Hannah were by no means the only Sisters who were instrumental in the spread of Christian feminist theology in Britain, and both they, and later other Sisters, especially those associated with the House at Brixton, pioneered inclusive liturgy and the use of inclusive language – at least regarding human beings – in the Office Book. Jenny Daggers notes the powerful relationship between the Movement for the Ordination of Women's aims, and the feminist liturgical expressions of the group Women in Theology, and the London-based St Hilda Community, of which both Sisters Hannah and Joyce were members. As I have suggested above, taking seriously the watchwords *lex orandi, lex credendi*, both these groups – Women in Theology finding local expressions around the country – developed liturgies that expressed and created the context for feminist recoveries and reworkings of the Christian faith. Sister Hannah wrote with her co-editor, Janet Morley, in the original Preface to *Celebrating Women*:

'Christians are formed by the way in which they pray'

So reads the Preface to the Alternative Service Book of the Church of England. The language we use has an enormous power to shape our perceptions: of ourselves, of our world, and of God. However, we inherit language for worship which, whether we are speaking of human beings or of God, overwhelmingly uses masculine pronouns and metaphors, as if these were neutral in their effect on those who pray.

Exclusive language is not a trivial matter, in church or out of it. It is both an accurate symptom of women's actual exclusion from many central forms of ministry and decision-making; and it is also a means of re-creating the attitudes which support such exclusion as 'normal' or within the purposes of God. Women can participate in this language, and speak the words that erase us, or we can choose to remain silent. Alternatively, we can struggle to create a language that includes us. *Celebrating Women* reflects the re-vision and new articulation of Christian truth that is being undertaken from the perspective of women. In this process, there is both pain and celebration; and there is an exploratory 'feel' to many of the pieces, which suggests that some of the hidden insights of women are only beginning to be expressed. (Morley, 1983, p. 2)

Sadly, this is an argument that needs to be repeated. The contribution that Sisters Joyce, Hannah and other Community of St Francis Sisters made to growing the awareness of such matters continues to be of significance.

Not all the work done by these Sisters was confined to the Anglican Church, however, nor did it always accord with church discipline. The work of Women in Theology was thoroughly ecumenical, and Sister Hannah in particular worked closely with Roman Catholic women's groups, including some of the powerful Religious Orders. Jenny Daggers notes in *The British Christian Women's Movement* an article by Hannah published in *Chrysalis* in 1987, in which Daggers states, 'she [Hannah] is now committed to building up women's Christian community, irrespective of Synod decisions'. Although some of her Community of St Francis Sisters found Sister Hannah's actions and writings very difficult, at the level of the Chapter the Minutes record support or at least acceptance of her stance (Daggers, 2002, p. 89).

Sister Hannah's words, quoted by Daggers, highlight the fact that this contribution to a generation of Christian feminists, of which I am also a member, was not only liturgical but embraced a different way of doing things, of running meetings, of reaching decisions, of activism that was celebratory and/or full of pain, and valued the singing and dancing of women. This feminist approach found its way into some of the structures of, for example, how House meetings were conducted. Again this was particularly so of the Brixton House, and it was not always appreciated by other Sisters, who at times expressed a desire that Brixton should be 'brought into line.'

Campaigners

It is not uncommon to see photographs of Community of St Francis Sisters at a variety of demonstrations, and these have included involvement with anti-nuclear movements in the 1980s, especially though Pax Christi, which seemed at least to some Sisters a better representation of the way of Jesus – and of St Francis – than the Campaign for Nuclear Disarmament (CND). Others, I should add, found Greenham Common's distinctively women's approach to peace appealing. More recently, involvement with Make Poverty History and a number of Christian Aid campaigns have been significant, as has environmental activism. Though all the Sisters with whom I have spoken wished to distance themselves from the sentimentality that has come to surround St Francis' understanding of the fraternity/sorority of all creatures, there is a real sense that this is an issue with which Franciscans need to be particularly involved. St Francis was, after all, declared Patron Saint of Environmentalists by Pope John Paul II in 1979, and St Francis rescues the reputation of Christianity in Lynn White's 1967 indictment of Christianity's impact on the environment. The Franciscan website refers to a recent example of this:

> On 17th June thousands came to the Houses of Parliament to speak to their MPs about climate change. Franciscans of the First and Third Orders were among them. Hilfield Friary Community members Jonathan and Daniel came with me with a coach group from Dorset, while Sr Maureen came from Metheringham and Br Michael Christoffer from Canterbury. Srs Sue and Gina had to come a very short way from Southwark. We were asked to speak up for the love of the good things our planet supports that could be spoilt by climate change – hence the title of the day, *Speak up for the love of …*
>
> The Climate Coalition, the group of charities and faith groups that organised the mass lobby claim around 9,000 constituents were there and that about 250 MPs were lobbied. Christian Aid is a member of the Coalition and had helped us to organise our trips. I saw people from Oxfam, A Rocha (which works closely with the Society of St Francis at Hilfield), CAFOD, and WWF among others who are in the coalition.

The lobby was timed to meet our MPs soon after the election, and in good time before the international conference on climate change in Paris in December. We were there to tell our MPs that it is vital that Britain does all it can to persuade the nations of the world to come to a deal to reduce greenhouse gas emissions – something they failed to do at the 2009 conference in Copenhagen, where I was part of a C/SSF team.

It was also on the eve of the publication of the Pope's Encyclical on climate change and its terrible consequences for our planet if we do not change our lifestyles. While the encyclical is unusually addressed to all human beings, not just to Catholics, it is of particular interest to Franciscans as it is entitled Laudato Si (Be Praised), the opening words of St Francis' Canticle of the Creatures.

We Franciscans and members of other Religious Orders who work within Justice and Peace Links began the day with an ecumenical service at the packed St Margaret's Westminster, a church where Politics and Prayer have mingled for centuries. The preacher, the Bishop of Salisbury, Rt Revd Nicholas Holtam, said: 'This is not just our individual concern. It is our Christian concern together as the church. It is the concern of people of all faiths. It is our human concern in solidarity with all people. The world is our home.' He praised the Encyclical, and also the Archbishop of Canterbury's Lambeth Declaration on Climate Change.

After the service we walked a short distance, in lovely sunny weather, to meet our MPs by the stretch of the Thames from the House of Commons and over the bridge to Lambeth Palace. Some of them arrived in rickshaws that the organisers had laid on. Our West Dorset MP, Oliver Letwin, gave us ten minutes and asked us to meet him again at home. After that the three of us from Hilfield visited a Muslim environmental stall at the interfaith area in Lambeth Park, and information stalls run by other charities in St John's, Smith Square.

Going home to Dorset, our coach met horrible traffic, and it took two hours to get from Westminster to Hammersmith. It was a reminder to me that even attending a climate lobby can involve emitting even more greenhouse gases.[7]

As well as these 'interventions', which have national and international implications and are part of the Community of St Francis' prophetic witness, there is much evidence of local intervention – I have already written of actions to improve the experience of pedestrians in a poor part of Leicester, and the House Reports which attest to Leonore's advocacy on behalf of Muslims in East London. These too might be seen as prophetic, and would certainly meet with the approval of John Hull, who argues: 'The works of justice and love lead us to Jesus Christ, and faith in Jesus Christ leads us to the works of justice and love, where "leads" means "implies" and "is equivalent to"' (Hull, 2014, p. 231).

Directors (Directees) and Retreat Leaders

That prayer is the lifeblood of the Community of St Francis is I trust obvious from all that I have written thus far, though it will, together with celibacy, receive some focused attention in Chapter 9. The business of prayer is also something with which Christian disciples struggle and flourish, about which they are perplexed or feel guilty. Seeking to understand the life of prayer, discerning God's call, not only in relation to major issues like life-changing vocations but in the minutiae of our daily lives, has become something with which help is increasingly sought among Christians and others. This ministry is not the vocation of all Sisters, but the unhierarchical approach that characterizes the Community of St Francis today has much in common with a style in spiritual direction that has come to prevail in many quarters, so that those who would formerly have called themselves 'directors' now often use words like 'companion, guide or accompanist'. Sisters of the Community of St Francis each have a 'director', normally someone from outside the Community who can help them discern and explore not only the life of prayer but the integrated life to which Sue refers as 'a lively expectation of finding Christ in actual human experience, in all of life, the ordinary, the appalling,

---

7 www.franciscans.org.uk/news-homepage/page/2.

and the wonderful'. Some Sisters use Brothers of the Community of St Francis in this capacity, and indeed for some who avail themselves of the sacrament of reconciliation, Brother may act as Confessor. Others use members of the Third Order for both these ministries but increasingly there is some sense that direction from outside the family of Franciscans may be beneficial.

For those Sisters who do offer this ministry (and for some it is a significant part of their lives), there is a focus on a ministry of listening, and although the resources of Franciscan spirituality are an obvious place to begin, there is a recognition that this may not be suitable for everyone, and a wide range of understandings may be brought into play. As for many Christians at this time, the Spiritual Exercises of St Ignatius are important for the spiritual practice and retreat of some Sisters, and a number offer individually guided retreats in this tradition. For others the centring prayer associated with Thomas Keating has been a focus of retreat and individual work.

Towards the end of its life (see Chapter 9), Compton Durville became focused as a house of hospitality for both rest and retreat, and this has been a ministry much missed since the closing of that House.

Early days at Compton Durville.

8
And Abroad

Day 26

The Brothers and Sisters must also refrain from all contemptuous thoughts one of another, and not seeking for pre-eminence must *regard others as better than themselves.* (Philippians 2.3)

The faults that they see in others must be subjects for prayer rather than criticism and they must be more diligent to *take the log out of their own eye* than *the speck out of their neighbour's eye.* (Matthew 7.5)

They must be ready not only gladly, *when invited, to go and sit down at the lowest place* (Luke 14.10), but rather of their own accord take it. Nevertheless, if entrusted with a work of which they feel incapable or unworthy, they must not shrink from accepting it on the plea of humility, but attempt it confidently through *the power (of Christ) made perfect in weakness.* (2 Corinthians 12.9)

In their relations also with those outside, the Brothers and Sisters must strive to show their Master's humility. They must welcome gladly all opportunities of humble service that come to them and never desire pre-eminence or praise. In particular they must resist the temptation to consider themselves superior to others because dedicated to a life of religion, realising how much greater often are the sacrifices and difficulties of those engaged in the ordinary professions of life and how much more nobly they face them.

(Principles Day 26)

As has, I think, been amply demonstrated in the last two chapters, the Community of St Francis, often in tandem with its Brother Community the Society of St Francis, was both pioneering and creative in its response to the requests that parishes and others brought them as they branched out. Discerning from among the many requests the voice of God's call, they were also responsive and creative in seeking to work *among* rather than *for* the people with whom they lived. This relational approach, a modern interpretation of St Francis' embracing of the leper and seeking out the poorest, knowing that with those people and in those places they would encounter Christ, was to continue to characterize their work. As well as working *among*, their work has focused on the empowerment of those who are marginalized and those who in other parts of the world longed to follow the way of Saints Francis and Clare also. It should be noted, however, that not all Sisters have felt called to travel, let alone sojourn in another country, and this is one of the areas where obedience has been costly for some.

This brief chapter seeks to tell something of the work of the Community of St Francis outside of the British Isles, and it does so briefly in the hope that at least some of those stories may be told more extensively elsewhere. The most long standing of the international Anglican Franciscan Provinces – that of the Americas – began in 1919 when the first Society of St Francis was established. The Community of St Francis in the Province of the Americas traces itself to 1974, and because of the way the European Sisters – that is those from the United Kingdom – and those of the United States of America have moved back and forth from time to time across the Atlantic, I intend to write a very short account of that relationship.

Brief mention will be made too of the Community of St Francis' work in Zambia, New Zealand (Aotearoa) and in Korea. This chapter, then, is a short 'Cook's Tour', which begins in Africa.

Fiwila

Chronologically the first example of the Community of St Francis' overseas mission and ministry was at the Anglican Mission Station in Fiwila in Zambia. The Brothers of the Society of St Francis had been working for some time at the Mission, 150 miles from the capital, Lusaka. The Mission comprised a church, school, small hospital and leprosarium. By 1967, when the request for the presence of members of the Community of St Francis was received, the school was being run by the Zambian government. The Brothers were to continue their pastoral work and give assistance with administration. The hospital was also run by Zambians but there was a shortage of nurses in that part of Zambia, and trained nurses were needed. The Brothers sent a request to the Community of St Francis, and when Agnes Mary discussed it with the Sisters she received a very enthusiastic response from two mature and long-standing members of the community, one of whom had been a missionary in India before joining the Community of St Francis.

Sisters Angela May and Veronica, Fiwila, Zambia.

They and their successors – seven Sisters in all – were later joined by some additional members of the Third Order who were nurses. The Sisters worked, one in the hospital and one in the leprosarium, until 1974. The Sisters struggled with the Chilala dialect, but provided important care and support for the Zambian staff. This was of especial significance when the village became a focus for those whose leprosy had become incurable, and the work of prevention and treatment moved to another centre. At this point the traditions of St Francis, and his care for lepers, and the Community's own tradition of caring for the dying, found expression in work that was at once demanding and redolent of the One who came not to be served but to serve, and to give his life. It also gave the Sisters concerned a real opportunity to meet Christ in the patients, and local people who served them also.

United States of America

Just as the work in Zambia was coming to a close, the Community of St Francis was invited to go to the USA, having received a number of aspirants and some who persevered as Sisters from the USA. The Society of St Francis in the Province of the Americas has as its strapline, 'Franciscan Brothers in the Episcopal Church since 1919', and as well as a number of Brothers in the USA, there were for a time two Brothers in Brazil, although these had always intended to be independent of the Society of St Francis. The United States Sisters of the Community of St Francis claim the history of the whole Community as their own, and then relate that 'In 1974 four Sisters came to San Francisco to found the American Province of CSF.'[8] In fact the invitation had been accepted in 1972, but it took some time for four Sisters to be identified as suitable and willing to go. It took even longer to arrange visas with 'permanent entry' and permission to work as well as reside. In fact, Sister Elizabeth recounts, this gave the four a chance to research extensively, and also to begin to come together as a coherent group. As ever, word had spread, and during this period an Episcopal priest who was visiting the UK made a request that the Sisters might work in his parish. However, the decision was made, appropriately, that the Sisters would go to the city named for Francis. There was already a Brothers' House in San Francisco, but too small to house five Sisters also – Elizabeth as Minister accompanied the four. Thus it was that the Sisters were initially received in the USA at Bishop's Ranch, a Diocesan Conference Centre that the US Brothers had just taken over. After a journey of 26 hours, the Sisters were driven by the

8 www.communitystfrancis.org/history.html.

Brothers to Bishop's Ranch, 80 miles north of San Francisco. This distance proved difficult, and so the Sisters soon found accommodation with their Roman Catholic Franciscan Sisters. The Franciscan Missionaries of Mary provided hospitality in the city, while Sister Elizabeth and the others searched for a suitable house. Eventually, it was possible to rent a suitable property on the edge of the 'Mission District' where Franciscan Friar Junipero de Sera and his Brothers had founded their settlement in the eighteenth century, and which has a mixed racial profile.

The current community website tells the story thus:

In 1974 four Sisters came to San Francisco to found the American Province of CSF. From time to time the Sisters in the USA have lived and worked elsewhere (notably running a small rural ministry for migrant farmworkers in Brentwood, CA, and a small urban house in Bethlehem, PA); however, the main work has been in San Francisco. The American Province Sisters decided against affiliation with a particular parish or institutional ministry, favouring the option of allowing each Sister to find a caring ministry suitable to her skills, interests and the needs which present themselves.

The initial ministries of the Sisters in San Francisco were meals-on-wheels, Church World Service (Southeast Asian refugee resettlement), an after-school tutoring program for disadvantaged children, hospital ministry, chaplaincy to the port of San Francisco, and volunteer work with the local church. True to our roots, from time to time the American Sisters have resorted to house cleaning to support ourselves.

At various times the original CSF ministry with the sick has been manifested in the form of hospital chaplaincy, home health care, and The Family Link, a hospital ministry for the loved ones of people with AIDS and other life-threatening illnesses. The old ministry with 'wayfarers' finds its new incarnational work with the homeless in San Francisco, especially through involvement with the local soup kitchen and food pantries. In addition to these caring ministries with the poor and needy, the Sisters offer retreats, spiritual direction and a small guest ministry.[9]

9 www.communitystfrancis.org/history.html.

New Zealand (Aotearoa)

The Brothers of the Society of St Francis had long had involvement in the Pacific, in Papua New Guinea and the Solomon Islands, in relationship with the Melanesian Brotherhood, and in the Australia/New Zealand Province. The work of Anglican Franciscanism in this latter Province was also to influence a number of women in that part of the world to try their vocations at the Anglican Franciscan Second Order Community of St Clare at Freeland in Oxfordshire.

Sister Maureen with Teresa and Jean, Auckland, NZ, 1990.

The first mention in the Minutes of the European Province was from 1984, when Sister Elizabeth spoke of a proposed venture to establish a Community in the New Zealand Province, which had been established among the Brothers of the Society of St Francis via the Pacific Province.

The Community of St Francis' Chapter strongly affirmed Sister Elizabeth's view that of God wanted the Community to go to New Zealand, and that being the case, God would provide the necessary Sisters, 'but that this required our common effort of faith'. Things moved swiftly and in 1985 Sisters Elizabeth and Teresa visited and found potential for a new community there. So in 1986, with Teresa as Minister the five Sisters – one New Zealander, two Australians and two English – started a house in Auckland, New Zealand. By 1990, however, it was clear that the group needed to be incorporated into the European Province. Reports from Auckland were nonetheless positive and the Sisters worked well together, making ecumenical work a focus of their ministries. Sister Phyllis became parish assistant in St Mark's Remuera, and a highlight of their ministry included providing hospitality for the first woman bishop in the Anglican Communion, the Rt Revd Penny Jamieson, who had been a friend of the Community for some time. Several women from New Zealand came over the years to test their vocation, but none stayed, and at the end of 1998 the house was closed and the remaining two Sisters returned to England.

South Korea

The experiment with having an outpost of the European Province in New Zealand (Aotearoa) meant that when the question of a Community of St Francis in South Korea arose, it was decided that the Sisters should be part of the European Province. This time the request came from Korea, and from some who were already living a Religious Life. Again, a group of men, encouraged and mentored by the Society of St Francis, had pioneered the Life as the Korean Franciscan Brotherhood. They later became part of the Society of St Francis. Brothers had pioneered Franciscanism in South Korea, a country with one of the fastest-growing churches, and also with a tradition of Buddhist monasticism that may have made Christian Religious Life more readily acceptable.

According to Sister Helen Julian's account:

In 1997 two existing members of a community in Korea felt called to live a more Franciscan life, and so left to found the Korean Franciscan

Sisterhood. They contacted CSF for support and advice, and in 2002 the two communities agreed a covenant, with Pamela Clare as first Mentor Sister to the new community. They made their first profession in 2001 and came to the UK to participate in CSF's centenary celebrations in 2005. The same year Beverley took over as Mentor Sister. In 2008 Frances and Jemma applied to the First Order Sisters' Chapter to become members of CSF; Chapter accepted their request and they were attached to the European Province. The following year they applied to make their life profession, and this took place in Gumi, South Korea on September 8th, 2009. Four Sisters – Joyce (Minister General), Helen Julian (Minister Provincial) and the two mentors, Pamela Clare and Beverley – travelled to Korea for this special occasion.

Religious gathered in the living room, Korea.

Sister Sue recounts her first visit to the Sisters in 2012:

In May I made my first visit to our Korean Sisters Frances and Jemma, staying at their home in Gumi, and with them, in Seoul, and at the SSF friary at Gangchon, where cleaning and repairs were well underway, following the explosion there ten days earlier.

It was a privilege to be with the Sisters and to share something of their community life. They currently occupy two small flats in adjacent blocks in downtown Gumi, but are in the process of building a convent in a nearby village, where they will be able to have guests and enable others to share in their life and worship more readily. Bishop Onesimus of Busan, who recently became Bishop Protector for CSF in Korea, is very appreciative of the Sisters and is providing support in various ways, including commending a fund-raising appeal among Korean Anglicans for their building project. He attended their Regional Chapter held in Seoul during my visit, and afterwards commented on his diocesan website that it had been a very beautiful and encouraging meeting! The Sisters are very involved in the life of the Anglican Church in Gumi, which celebrated its tenth anniversary while I was there, and also more widely. They are obviously held in high regard, and both exercise a significant pastoral ministry alongside their other work.

It is surely a joyful part of my task as Minister to visit the Korean Sisters each year. We hope that by the time of my next visit Frances and Jemma will have moved to Il-Seon-Ri, and will temporarily have fitted everything essential into one new building there while the second is being constructed. These are exciting and challenging times for the Sisters, and they very much value our support and prayers.

The Sisters in Gumi, South Korea, have, after a long search, bought a house. Built in the traditional Korean style, it is in a village just outside the city of Gumi. Once some necessary renovation has taken place, the Sisters will be able to leave the rented flats which have been their home since the community started, while continuing their work with the church and other projects in Gumi ...

Sister Sue attended the 'ground-breaking' ceremony in August 2013, just before the Minsters' Meeting in Seoul, and Gina and Sue attended the Blessing of the new convent in May 2014.

Ground-breaking ceremony, Korea.

My visit to Frances and Jemma in Korea included the excellent ground-breaking ceremony for the Sisters' new convent in Il-Seon-Ri, on 8 August. It was good to renew contacts with Gumi church and with the children's project there which Frances leads. The Sisters continue to live and work well together, and with the SSF Brothers at Chuncheon in Seoul diocese, and are held in very high regard in their own diocese and more widely. They also have supportive links with local Catholic religious, Franciscans and others. The recent C/SSF Ministers Meeting in Seoul, and its attendant publicity, has undoubtedly helped to raise the profile of our Korean Sisters and Brothers in Korea, and reminded the church of their context as part of SSF worldwide. (from Sister Sue's report to Francistide 2013 Chapter)

The Blessing Service on 16th May [2014] was attended by over 100 people including Gina and me, SSF Brothers, and other Religious, and was an inspiring and joyful occasion. On 22nd a church group of around 30 visited the house, with Frances and Jemma leading Taize prayer in the chapel. Having a traditional Korean style house makes a big impression on people, and visitors are most impressed by the beauty and simplicity of the place. The Sisters are well loved and respected in the Korean church, and are building relationships with the local village community. (From Sister Sue's report to Pentecost 2014 chapter)

The news of August 2015 was that with the Community's full support Frances has been recommended for training for ordination to the priesthood, by the church in Korea.

More on the Gumi Convent

The Korean Sisters write:

In the Gyeongsangbukdo Province of South Korea, in the Diocese of Busan, at the outskirts of Gumi, there is a beautiful and peaceful traditional Korean village where in 2014 we built a traditional Korean-style convent. Il-Seon-Ri is a model village, formed according to the principles of Confucian thought, and in this place the Korean Franciscan Sisters have put down roots among the villagers, working to enable the budding forth of a new way of living that allows Confucianism and Christianity to co-exist side by side. To people thirsty for rest and peace, tired out by the complexities of modern life, the Sisters offer a warm welcome and friendship, prayer and the opportunity for spiritual guidance. Through working for the welfare of young people and the production of clerical vestments, the Korean Sisters are forming links with the church and the local community; and by actively welcoming those who wish to visit the convent, the 'open days' of Tuesday to Saturday provide an opportunity to share in the Daily Office and the day-to-day life of the convent. With two guest rooms, the outer traditional form of the building is complemented by an interior with the comforts of modern living, and the guests are welcome to use the convent chapel, living room, garden, and common spaces of the house.

9
Endings and Renewals,
Whys and Wherefores

Day 14

Praise and prayer constitute the atmosphere in which the Brothers
and Sisters must strive to live. They must endeavour to maintain a
constant recollection of the presence of God and of the unseen world.
An ever-deepening devotion to Christ is the hidden source of all their
strength and joy. He is for them the One all-lovely and adorable, God
incarnate, crucified and risen, whose love is the inspiration of service
and the reward of sacrifice.

Day 15

That their union with this Lord and Master may be ever renewed and
strengthened, the Brothers and Sisters unite in offering daily before
God the memorial of his death and passion and feeding often upon
his sacrificial life. The Holy Eucharist is the centre round which their
life revolves. It is above all the heart of their prayer life.

The time of morning prayer is the preparation of mind and spirit for
entrance within the sanctuary. The meditation which follows later is
the opportunity for quiet tryst with him who through the sacrament,
is present inwardly, and for feeding on him in the heart by faith with
thanksgiving.

The services of intercession and thanksgiving are times when those
who have been thus joined with him in communion and meditation
may plead with God in sure reliance on his promise: *If you abide*

in me, and my words abide in you, ask for whatever you wish, and it will be done for you (John 15.7), and also thank him for continuous experience of its fulfilment.

The evening office is the renewed offering of praise and prayer to the same Lord at the end of the day's work, and in its closing silence the hearts of all are together steeped afresh in the peace of that inward uncreated light which, as the shadows of life deepen, abides unchanged. Compline is the Master's blessing of protection and peace.

(Principles Days 14 and 15)

Leaving Compton Durville

Long the home of the community of St Francis if not formally its mother House, there is, for the most part, a great deal of affection for Compton Durville, and its work. The archives, however, also record a great deal of frustration, and the 'taint of Compton Durville' is a phrase that occurs more than once. The Manor House at Compton Durville was, and is, undoubtedly beautiful, and set in a quiet country lane the convent and its guest house bestriding a single-track road, one can become quite romantic about it. The Manor House is of golden, weathered Bath stone and its steps come to greet you if you drive or walk from the direction of South Petherton. It is also large and cumbersome, and not what estate agents call 'well appointed'. With a lot of money and time it might have been transformed into a comfortable house, but Franciscans have other priorities, not least relating to money, and so it became a burden. Not only was the fabric a huge responsibility, but the frustrations of keeping it in good repair – though the community of St Francis was responsible only for its interior upkeep – took large amounts of time, which many Sisters felt might have been better spent on ministry that more directly seemed to represent their charism.

The nursing home having closed, Compton Durville focused on hospitality, groups and especially individuals who visited the house for spiritual direction and retreats, more or less formal. But against this undoubtedly valuable ministry stood for some Sisters a commitment to urban mission and solidarity with the urban poor, and though rural poverty is a significant factor of living in the country, South Petherton and its environs were not for the most part deprived.

There was also the garden, the terraced garth where Sisters' cremated remains were buried, and the other gardens, on one side of the road extensive and at a very steep angle, on the other simply extensive. Although Sister Phyllis instigated gardening days and retreats where people visited for reflection, and which helped enormously with the upkeep of the grounds, there was always gardening to be done. Both house and garden were formidable.

There was also the issue of 'taint', and for some of the Sisters, Compton Durville had come to symbolize their most miserable years in community. For some it represented 'dead time' of what felt like domestic servitude, while, as some thought, more important work went on elsewhere. There were feelings of almost entrapment – the remoteness of the House was a problem even after a car was purchased. Not everyone shared these views, but undoubtedly Compton Durville had become a behemoth. As one Sister put it, 'it felt like hands were tied' by the demands of the building.

Sister Helen Julian writes:

In 2008 the Sisters of the European Province began a period of reflection and review of their life, especially through the Sisters' Meeting 2009, which focused on 'our gifts and skills, our existing houses, and our hopes and dreams for the future'. As a result of this process a Working Group of five Sisters was mandated to explore alternatives to the House at Compton Durville, which it was recognized had become too large for us to manage. The Candlemas Chapter 2010 agreed to purchase a redundant vicarage in the village of Metheringham, Lincolnshire; and to close the House at Compton Durville. The House closed for ministry in May of that year, and the final Sisters left in October. The handover to the Number One Trust was finally concluded in April 2011. A large number of Sisters moved in the course of 2010; only one House was left unchanged by the end of the year.

There was undoubtedly some sense of regret, perhaps mostly among those who visited the house rather than those who lived there. But the tone of Sister Helen Julian's account – perhaps because of its brevity – does not do justice to the energy which, once the House was left, and in itself that was tremendous work, began to emerge. The decision to find another, very much smaller rural House of prayer, more accessible for transport, resulted in the purchase – rents being now a major expense because of the British housing market – of delightful clergy house in Metheringham, where the massive tau cross from Compton Durville now hangs on a gable end. There was an air, I felt at least, of liberation in leaving Compton Durville.

And there was celebration. In 2005, as part of the centenary celebrations, there was a gathering of members of the Community who had left: Sister Beverley's 'Fourth Order of St Francis'. I am told that it had the atmosphere of a gaudy without the posh frocks and the competitiveness. Certainly there was a lot of 'catching up' and laughter.

The final Eucharist at Compton Durville was also celebratory. People gathered from all 'four' orders, including some who had not been back to Compton Durville since they left the Community. There was a touch of a garden party about it all, excellent food, and apple juice hand-pressed by Sister Damien of the Second Order, who had once been Sister Wendy of the Community of St Francis. After the Eucharist people lounged about, reminiscing. There was a great deal of hugging, of walking through the gardens, and of laughter.

And the Eucharist was just that, the life of the Community of St Francis, at Compton Durville and beyond, lifted up, fractured, broken, and with enormous gratitude for all that had been: 'This is my body broken, for you, this is my life blood offered for you, which has been, and is, and shall be, transformed, and transforming, into the stuff of God's kingdom.'

Dag Hammarskjöld wrote: 'For all that has been – thanks! For all that shall be – Yes.'

Totality

> You might think a total eclipse would have no colour. The word 'eclipse' comes from the ancient Greek *ekleipsis*, 'a forsaking, quitting, abandonment.' Yet people who experience total eclipse are moved to such strong descriptions of its vacancy and void that this itself begins to take on colour. (Carson, 2006, p. 149)

There is something gloriously interwoven in the doctrines of the incarnation, of the Eucharist and of ecclesiology, and that is the body of Christ. Some theologians – I think of Grace Jantzen and Sallie McFague particularly – want to extend this to embrace the whole of creation as the body of God. In creation and incarnation, in Eucharist and church, God is embodied. At the heart of Franciscan life is a sense of totality, of inclusion, that there are no dualistic or binary categories in Christ, all shall be restored, all is being transformed, all will – in due course – be glorified.

In Sandra Schneiders' core text *Selling All*, St Francis and St Clare receive barely a mention, though neither do many important historical figures. What Schneiders does summarize is, however, one important key to understanding the charism of the Community of St Francis (and in this she does refer both to St Francis and to St Clare). As well as the desire literally to 'sell all' and follow Christ in absolute poverty, preaching the gospel to all creatures was integral to the vision of Francis of Assisi and Dominic Gurzman and other founders of male mendicant orders, but also to women like Clare of Assisi who, though necessarily cloistered, saw her life and that of her Sisters as intrinsically apostolic, a sharing of prayer and vision, and also by absolute poverty and insecurity, in the itinerant life of male Franciscans (Schneiders, 2001, p. 254).

Certainly it is possible to see St Clare though the lens of poverty, and, I would argue, it is possible to see the Religious vows of obedience and celibacy through this lens also. All three vows, it seems to me, partake of the *kenosis* to which I have referred before and to which Christians, and traditionally especially Religious, are called:

Let the same mind be in you that was in Christ Jesus,
who, though he was in the form of God,
did not regard equality with God
as something to be exploited,
but emptied himself,
taking the form of a slave,
being born in human likeness.
And being found in human form,
he humbled himself
and became obedient to the point of death –
even death on a cross. (Philippians 2.5–8)

It is also possible to see the Religious vows through the lens of celibacy, and it is to a particular interpretation of that virtue that I turn in this final chapter. It is easy to see the attraction of poverty when it is made of one's own volition, and when it is practised in a community setting, though perhaps more difficult for Franciscans who do not often own property, and may therefore be subject to the whims of landlords. In truth Religious poverty, even in Franciscan settings, is not usually practised as absolute poverty nowadays, though at least one of the Society of St Francis Brothers slept rough for a time in 'Cardboard City' in London in the 1980s. Poverty, even for Franciscans, has become simplicity, and, as such, in our aspirational consumer society it offers a real prophetic witness. Accounting for (almost) every penny may not be miserly but a sharing of the limitations of the poor, as might be refusing to have a credit card, or mending things in a culture where things broken are thrown away and replaced. This can be attractive.

Again in a society where choice is often portrayed as paramount – even in a land of universal health care our politicians say we should have the choice of which hospital to attend – it may be that the accountability of listening to God, ourselves and others that obedience implies has its attractions. Again this may be prophetic; it is certainly counter-cultural.

Celibacy, however, is usually interpreted in a negative way. It is a vow that is usually described in terms of what one may not be or do: be married, have a family, have sex. This too may be seen as counter-cultural: where bodies – especially women's bodies – are held cheaply, a life without sex that is rich and fulfilling is indeed a prophetic sign. Like the other Religious vows, however, this vow is a matter of calling, of gift, of volition, and I would not at all wish to defend compulsory celibacy.

There are few medieval portrayals of St Clare of Assisi, and the one famous 'portrait' of her is now generally believed to be of Agnes of Prague, but many of the medieval portrayals of the Blessed Virgin Mary depict her in a walled garden, with a gate firmly shut. However one regards this imagery, and it is symbolically graphic, the idea of being 'walled about with God' is a fascinating one. For not only does it imply enclosure, but containment, and I believe a containment that is redolent with freedom.

Flannery O'Connor was quoted by the British author David Almond on *Open Book*, BBC Radio 4, 18 June 2015, as saying: 'The imagination is not free, it is bound, but only when you've found the boundaries of your own imagination do you then, paradoxically, become free.'

The paradoxes of the Christian life and of Christian theology are many, and can be abused, not least when the powerful declare that the containment of the powerless is for their own good, as they have in many contexts and perhaps from the beginning of time. Yet as Rowan Williams writes:

> we need to express some sense of this strange fact that our language doesn't 'keep up' with the multiplicity and interrelatedness and elusiveness of truth. In such a setting, we utter paradoxes not to mystify or avoid problems, but precisely to *stop* ourselves making things easy by pretending that some awkward or odd feature of our perception isn't really there. We speak in paradoxes because we have to speak in a way that keeps a question alive. (Williams, 1995, pp. 99–100)

It is the paradox of containment that it sets us free, of celibacy that it is about generosity. And looking at frescos of the virgin in the garden, I do have a vision of the Blessed Virgin with a smile on her face and a key in her possession.

In *Selling All*, Sandra Schneiders sees the vow of celibacy as very particular to Religious Life, and it is. Though celibacy may be a gift (or a fact of life given to others), it is seldom the subject of vows. Schneiders regards it as being neither universal nor implied in our baptismal vows in the way that poverty and obedience, interpreted as thoughtful accountability, are. Celibacy, by contrast,

> is a vocation to a particular state of life that governs everything else in their life the way marriage governs the whole life of the person who marries. In other words the person is not simply choosing to practice a particular form of chastity, namely, that of the unmarried, but to construct her life or his life, in its totality, in a particular way for the sake of the Reign of God. (Schneiders, 2001, p. 126)

This is certainly the witness of some of the Sisters of the Society of St Francis with whom I have spoken, and this is different from the impression given in, for example, Mumm's consideration of why Religious Life was so powerful a force during the time of its rediscovery in the Anglican Church. Neither is it, I think, a rather simple exchange, or availability, that to abandon the love of one particular person frees one to love everyone, or at least a lot of people, as is often argued.

What I want to suggest is slightly different, and in doing so I hope to bring to the fore again the prophetic nature of this vow, and of the Religious Life generally. Like Schneiders, I want to suggest that the vow of celibacy is about the whole of life, but unlike her I also want to suggest that the vow of celibacy, like those of poverty and indeed obedience, is, if not implied, a distillation of the call of all Christian disciples.

Earlier in this book I referred to a sense I had, and have, that Christian disciples, in all conditions of life may have something of importance to learn from the paradigm of being an Apostolic Sister. In an at once secular and religiously plural society, I wonder whether the universal Christian call to be 'a holy people, a royal priesthood' (1 Peter 2.9) is not a call to be like Apostolic Sisters, who take on as we perhaps daily are invited to, at least in 'thought and word and deed,' vows of poverty, obedience and celibacy. For most Christian disciples this celibacy will indeed be some form of chastity, but not, I believe, chastity as opposed to adultery or promiscuity – another debate altogether – but chastity, which like celibacy, is about totality.

In his popular book, *How to become a Saint*, Jack Bernard continually reiterates the business of integrity and singleness of heart. These are, of course, words redolent of celibacy: integrity has its etymological roots in words that speak of being 'intact' or 'whole'; singleness, though nowadays most frequently suggesting being unmarried, has as its etymological roots the idea of being 'simple' in the sense of one, undivided. Both these words suggest the living of a life of what psychotherapists call 'congruence', the compatibility of evidence and argument, of word and action. One might even associate this with 'virtue': Stanley Hauerwas' community of character comprises disciples whose lives, by the grace of God, are or seek to be congruent – at least to some extent – with the values of the gospel.

As Diadochus of Photikē wrote: 'All of us are made according to the image of God. But only those who through great love have enslaved their own freedom to God are in his likeness. When we no longer belong to ourselves, then we are similar to him who has reconciled us to himself through love.'

This kind of 'celibacy' or life focused towards God in Christ and in the power of the Holy Spirit, is something to which I believe we are all called as disciples, and to which apostolic Religious Life, not least in the Franciscan tradition with it strong sense of poverty, is both paradigm and distillation. Solemn vows make this distilled and focused, and binding, but I would not suggest that the vows implicit, and sometimes explicit, among ordinary disciples are any less serious or significant.

The life in which the Blessed Trinity is all in all, is also a life of totality. And it is relational, as St Francis suggests, with all people, especially those who are despised and rejected; with all creatures and with all creation. This is not a life where focus on God means that one can ignore or neglect God's creation; rather, to quote Dietrich Bonheoffer:

> What I mean is that God wants us to love him eternally with all our hearts – not in such a way as to injure or weaken our earthly love, but to provide a kind of *cantus firmus* to which all other melodies provide the counterpoint. (Bonhoeffer, 1997, p. 301)

As we embrace the life of totality, of the undivided (simple) way of God, our integrity or congruence is bound up in the integration of all life. There is no more a holy day or a less holy day, except as one is a distillation of the other, allowing us to focus better on the holiness of every day. There is no more sacred and profane. As J. Neville Ward writes, 'all that happens is to be received as a word from God', and all that happens is to achieve a response according to the way of Jesus. And that does not mean passively, nor does it suggest a blandness with which some Saints are tarnished, but may be anger, may be protest, may be a strategy to change; it may even be a refusal. This particular word from God may require a *No pasarán*: we will not accept what society says of the poor or disabled, the refugees, those who follow the way of Islam.

In his excellent 1985 book *What Prevents Adult Christians from Learning?*, John Hull suggests that for some Christians the journey from work to home – for those who are privileged to have paid work – is a transition from competition and rivalry, impatience with weakness and sometimes aggression, to a more gentle, supportive and overtly Christian persona. Some of this is what is suggested by Elizabeth Stuart, in the article to which I have already referred, where she describes discipleship 'collapsing into family life' (Stuart, 1999). This is a domesticating of Christianity; it denies its place in the public sphere, its prophetic voice. The way of totality, of the undivided way, does not allow for such change of persona, for it undermines the way of Jesus. This may result in some uncomfortable moments in competitive places of work, but also asserts the primacy of God's reign.

I want to suggest that this kind of universal 'celibacy', or integrity, the focusing of all our lives on God, living totality, is prayer. Every minute we are turned Godward, consciously or unconsciously (and for most of us it will be the latter most of the time), we are adopting the demeanour of prayer. St Francis, who did this better than most, said he became prayer. As Sister Liz said of presiding at the Eucharist as a Franciscan: 'it feels more prayed, the Holy Spirit takes over'. Is this what is meant by 'the prayer prays me'?

The Church has long recognized that its work is the work of God, and

---

that is not to suggest that there is something exclusively Godlike about the church, or that nothing and no one else can mirror God's image. Indeed the Church often seems simply to provide barriers to God's generous love. But what I want to emphasize here is that living totality is the *opus Dei* – the work of God. The paradox of the way of totality is that it is the work of grace in creation. As we turn to this way, we find that we are indeed mysteriously participating in the life of God, and that life is whole, inclusive and is love, 'unbounded and eternal'.

Thus as we offer ourselves to this work, to sharing the way of St Francis, *il poverello*, of Jesus who was the divine embodied but became a nobody, we will find that the work of God will happen in us. It is as if, to quote the Methodist covenant prayer, 'I [really] am no longer my own but yours'. In this the idea of a life given totally, focused totally, undivided, of being apostolic, becomes a paradigm. And I do believe that my life as a baptized person means that this life compels me, demands of me, everything. I suppose by that I mean that God compels, God demands. I have in mind here a poem by R. S. Thomas in which God is portrayed as a raptor who might get God's claws into us. Yet I am free: though God is compelling I am not compelled, I am free to decide, as the covenant prayer goes on: 'I freely and wholeheartedly yield all things to your pleasure and disposal.' In giving myself unreservedly to God, I am set free.

As a baptized person, like a Franciscan Sister, I am called to live a life in solidarity with Christ, who is known in the poor and marginalized. As a baptized person, like a Franciscan Sister, I am called to live a life of accountability, a listening for the word of God, knowing it comes to me in every situation, and living its call. As a baptized person I am called to live my life as an integrated whole, undivided, 'to construct her life or his life, in its totality, in a particular way for the sake of the Reign of God' (Schneiders, 2001, p. 126).

This sense of the totality of things, of all life becoming prayer, God's prayer in us, is compelling. Within the vows or out of them, as the incarnate One becomes for us the bread and wine, and as we become 'Christ's body here on earth', the Franciscan embrace of all creation, all experience, rings in our ears:

Tue so le laude, la gloria e l'honore et onne benedictione.

Ad Te solo, Altissimo, se konfano,

et nullu homo ène dignu te mentouare.

Laudato sie, mi Signore cum tucte le Tue creature,

spetialmente messor lo frate Sole,

lo qual è iorno, et allumini noi per lui.

Et ellu è bellu e radiante cum grande splendore:

de Te, Altissimo, porta significatione.

Laudato si, mi Signore, per sora Luna e le stelle:

in celu l'ài formate clarite et pretiose et belle.

Laudato si, mi Signore, per frate Uento

et per aere et nubilo et sereno et onne tempo,

per lo quale, a le Tue creature dài sustentamento.

Laudato si, mi Signore, per sor'Acqua,

la quale è multo utile et humile et pretiosa et casta.

Laudato si, mi Signore, per frate Focu,

per lo quale ennallumini la nocte:

ed ello è bello et iucundo et robustoso et forte.

Laudato si, mi Signore, per sora nostra matre Terra,

la quale ne sustenta et gouerna,

et produce diuersi fructi con coloriti fior et herba.

Laudato si, mi Signore, per quelli ke perdonano per lo Tuo amore

et sostengono infirmitate et tribulatione.

Beati quelli ke 'l sosterranno in pace,

ka da Te, Altissimo, sirano incoronati.

Laudato si mi Signore, per sora nostra Morte corporale,

da la quale nullu homo uiuente pò skappare:

guai a quelli ke morrano ne le peccata mortali;

beati quelli ke trouarà ne le Tue sanctissime uoluntati,

ka la morte secunda no 'l farrà male.

Laudate et benedicete mi Signore et rengratiate

e seruiteli cum grande humilitate.

Notes: so=sono, si=sii (you are), mi=mio, ka=perché, u replaces v, sirano=saranno[10]

---

10 https://en.wikipedia.org/wiki/canticle_of_the_Sun.

For Peace and for Good

English Translation

Most high, all powerful, all good Lord!
All praise is yours, all glory, all honor, and all blessing.
To you, alone, Most High, do they belong.
No mortal lips are worthy to pronounce your name.
Be praised, my Lord, through all your creatures,
especially through my lord Brother Sun,
who brings the day; and you give light through him.
And he is beautiful and radiant in all his splendor!
Of you, Most High, he bears the likeness.
Be praised, my Lord, through Sister Moon and the stars;
in the heavens you have made them bright, precious and beautiful.
Be praised, my Lord, through Brothers Wind and Air,
and clouds and storms, and all the weather,
through which you give your creatures sustenance.
Be praised, my Lord, through Sister Water;
she is very useful, and humble, and precious, and pure.
Be praised, my Lord, through Brother Fire,
through whom you brighten the night.
He is beautiful and cheerful, and powerful and strong.
Be praised, my Lord, through our Sister Mother Earth,
who feeds us and rules us,
and produces various fruits with colored flowers and herbs.
Be praised, my Lord, through those who forgive for love of you;
through those who endure sickness and trial.
Happy those who endure in peace,
for by you, Most High, they will be crowned.
Be praised, my Lord, through our Sister Bodily Death,
from whose embrace no living person can escape.
Woe to those who die in mortal sin!
Happy those she finds doing your most holy will.
The second death can do no harm to them.
Praise and bless my Lord, and give thanks,
and serve him with great humility.[11]

---

11 Translated by Bill Barrett from the Umbrian text of the Assisi codex – www2.webster.
edu/~barrett/canticle.htm.

References and Further Reading

Abbott, Walter M., 1965, *The Documents of Vatican II*, London: Geoffrey Chapman.

Allchin, A. M., 1958, *The Silent Rebellion: Anglican Religious Communities 1845–1900*, London: SCM Press.

Allchin, A. M., 1971, The Theology of the Religious Life, Oxford: SLG Press.

Allchin, A. M., 1977, *Solitude and Communion: Papers on the Hermit Life*, Oxford: SLG Press.

Armstrong, Regis J., 1982, *Francis and Clare: The Complete Works*, Mahwah, NJ: Paulist Press.

Armstrong, Regis J., 2006, *The Lady: Clare of Assisi, Early Documents*, New York: New City Press.

Armstrong, Regis J., 2006, *True Joy: The Wisdom of Francis and Clare*, Mahwah, NJ: Paulist Press.

Armstrong, Regis J. and Peterson, Ingrid J., 2010, *The Franciscan Tradition*, Collegeville, MN: Liturgical Press.

Bartoli, Marco, 2011, *Clare of Assisi*, London: Darton, Longman & Todd.

Bernard, Jack, 2007, *How To Become A Saint: A Beginner's Guide*, London: SPCK.

Bodo, Murray, 1973, *Francis: The Journey and the Dream*, Cincinnati, OH: St Anthony Messenger.

Bodo, Murray, 2015, *Enter Assisi: An Invitation to Franciscan Spirituality*, Cincinnati, OH: Franciscan Media.

Boff, Leonardo, 1982, *Saint Francis: A Model for Human Liberation*, London: SCM Press.

Bonhoeffer, Dietrich, 1997, *Letters and Papers from Prison: The Enlarged Edition*, ed. Eberhard Bethge, New York: Touchstone (letter to Bethge written from Tegel prison, 21 May 1944).

Brooke, Rosalind B., 1975, *The Coming of the Friars: Historical Problems*, New York: Barnes & Noble.

Brother Lawrence, 1982, *The Practice of the Presence of God*, trans. E. M. Blaiklock, London: Hodder & Stoughton.

Carmody, Maurice, 2008, *St Francis of Assisi and His Influence Since the Thirteenth Century*, London: Athena Press.

Carney, Margaret, 1993, *The First Franciscan Woman: Clare of Assisi and Her Form of Life*, Cincinnati, OH: Franciscan Media.

Carson, Anne, 2006, 'Totality', in *Decreation*, London: Jonathan Cape.

Cirino, Andre, 1995, *Franciscan Solitude*, New York: Franciscan Institute Publications.

Cron, In Morgan, 2013, *Chasing Francis: A Pilgrim's Tale*, Grand Rapids, MI: Zondervan.

Daggers, Jenny, 2002, *The British Christian Women's Movement: The Rehabilitation of Eve*, London: Routledge.

de Caussade, Jean Pierre, 1981, *The Sacrament of the Present Moment*, trans. Kitty Muggeridge, London: Collins.

Delio, Ilia, 2011, *Living in the Spirit of St Francis*, Cincinnati, OH: St Anthony Messenger Press.

Delio, Ilia, 2011, *The Humility of God: A Franciscan Perspective*, Cincinnati: St Anthony Messenger Press.

Dunstan, Petà, 1997, *This Poor Sort: A History of the European Province of the Society of St Francis*, London: Darton, Longman & Todd.

Dunstan, Petà, 2009, *The Labour of Obedience: The Benedictines – A History of Pershore, Nashdom and Elmore*, Norwich: Canterbury Press.

Elizabeth CSF, 1981, *Corn of Wheat: The Life and History of the Community of St Francis*, Oxford: Becket Publications.

Foley, Leonard and Weigel, Joyian, 2016, *Live Like Franciscans: Reflections on Franciscan Life in the World*, Cincinnati, OH: Franciscan Media.

Frances, Teresa, OSC, 1993, *Living the Incarnation: Praying with Francis and Clare*, London: Darton, Longman & Todd.

Frances, Teresa, OSC, 1995, *The Living Mirror: Reflections on Clare of Assisi*, London: Darton, Longman & Todd.

References and Further Reading

Hammarskjöld, Dag, 1964, trans Leif Sjöberg and W. H. Auden, London: Faber & Faber.

Helen Julian, CSF, 2001, *Living the Gospel: The Spirituality of St Francis and St Clare*, Oxford: Bible Reading Fellowship.

Hennessy, Peter, 1993, *Never Again: Britain 1945–1951*, London: Vintage.

Henzler, Ingrid, 2012, *The God Seekers: The Life of the Franciscans Today*, Corby: Watermark Publishing.

House, Adrian, 2014, *Francis of Assisi: A Revolutionary Life*, Mahwah, NJ: Paulist Press.

Hull, John, 1985, *What Prevents Adult Christians from Learning?*, London: SCM Press.

Hull, John, 2014, *Towards a Prophetic Church: A Study of Christian Mission*, London: SCM Press.

Hutton, Edward, 1926, *The Franciscans in England 1224–1538*, London: Constable & Co.

Jordan, Patricia, 2008, *An Affair of the Heart: A Biblical and Franciscan Journey*, Leominster: Gracewing.

McFague, Sallie, 1993, The Body of God: An Ecological Theology, Minneapolis, MN: Augsburg Press.

McNamarra, Jo Ann Kay, 1996, *Sisters in Arms: Catholic Nuns through Two Millennia*, Cambridge, MA: Harvard University Press.

Methodist Worship Book, 1999, Norwich: Methodist Publishing House.

Monti, Dominic, 2011, *Francis and His Brothers: A Popular History of the Franciscan Friars*, Cincinnati, OH: St Anthony Messenger Press.

Morley, Janet, 1983, Foreword, in Hannah Ward, Jennifer Wild and Janet Morley, *Celebrating Women*, London: SPCK.

Mueller, Joan, 2008, *The Privilege of Poverty: Clare of Assisi, Agnes of Prague and the Struggle for a Franciscan Rule for Women*, University Park, PA: Pennsylvania State University Press.

Mumm, Susan, 1999, *Stolen Daughters, Virgin Mothers: Anglican Sisterhoods in Victorian Britain*, London: Leicester University Press.

Nicholson, Virginia, 2008, *Singled Out: How Two Million Women Survived Without Men After the First World War*, London: Penguin.

Palmer, Bernard, 2012, *Men of Habit: The Franciscan Ideal in Action*, Norwich: Canterbury Press.

Pearson, Kate, 2012, 'Then and Now, There and Here: Does the Franciscan tradition as found in the Writings of Angela of Foligno yield Insights for Women's Pioneer Ministry in Weoley Castle?' unpublished MA dissertation, Birmingham: The Queen's Foundation.

Pitchford, Susan R., 2006, *Following Francis: The Franciscan Way for Everyone*, New York: Moorhouse Publishing.

Ramon SSF, 2008, *Franciscan Spirituality*, London: SPCK.

Robson, Michael, 1997, *St Francis of Assisi: The Legend and the Life*, London: Continuum.

Robson, Michael, 2006, *Franciscans in the Middle Ages*, Woodbridge: Boydell Press.

Rohr, Richard, 2002, *Hope Against Darkness: The Transforming Vision of St Francis in the Age of Anxiety*, Cincinnati, OH: St Anthony Messenger Press.

Rohr, Richard, 2014, *Eager to Love: The Alternative Way of Francis of Assisi*, London: Hodder & Stoughton.

Schneiders, Sandra, IHM, 2001, *Selling All: Commitment, Consecrated Celibacy and Community in Catholic Religious Life*, Mahwah, NJ: Paulist Press.

Short, William J., 1999, *Poverty and Joy: The Franciscan Tradition*, London: Darton, Longman & Todd.

Spoto, Donald, 2003, *Reluctant Saint: The Life of Francis of Assisi*, London: Penguin.

Starr, Mirabai, 2004, 'Teresa of Avila and Mirabai Starr', in *Interior Castle*, New York: Riverhead Books.

Strauss, David Friedrich (1846), *The Life of Jesus Critically Examined*, trans. George Eliot, Whitefish, MT: Kessinger Publishing.

Stuart, Elizabeth, 1999, 'Sexuality: The View from the Font', in *Theology and Sexuality* 6:11.

Sweeney, Jon M., 2013, *Francis and Clare: A True Story*, Brewster, MA: Paraclete Press.

Sweeney, Jon M., 2015, *Francis of Assisi: His Life, The Complete Writings and The Little Flowers*, Brewster, MA: Paraclete Press.

Talbot, John Michael, 1985, *Lover and the Beloved: The Way of Franciscan Prayer*, New York: Crossroad Publishing.

Thompson, Augustine, 2012, *Francis of Assisi: A New Biography*, New York, Cornell University Press.

Underhill, Evelyn, 1991 (1928), 'Spiritual Life of the Preacher', in *Life as Prayer and Other Writings of Evelyn Underhill*, Harrisburg, PA: Morehouse.

Webb, Elizabeth, CSF, 1998, 'Empowering Community: Revisioning Participation in Structures of Authority in three Anglican Religious Orders for Women', unpublished MTh dissertation, Oxford: Westminster College.

White, Lynn, Jr., 1967, 'The Historical Roots of Our Ecological Crisis', *Science* 15:3767, pp. 12037.

Williams, Barrie, 1982, *The Franciscan Revival in the Anglican Communion*, London: Darton, Longman & Todd.

Williams, Rowan Clare, 2011, *A Condition of Complete Simplicity: Franciscan Wisdom for Today's World. Franciscan Wisdom for Everyday*, London: Canterbury Press.

Williams, Rowan Clare, 1995, A *Ray of Darkness*, Cambridge, MA: Cowley Publications.

Appendix 1

Record of Sisters of the Community of St Francis

Living and Departed CSF Sisters (October 2015)

Living	Profession
European Province	
Elizabeth	1957
Gwenfryd Mary	1967
Gina (Community of St John the Baptist)	1969
Transferred to CSF 1992	
Joyce	1973
Hilary	1977
Jannafer	1974
Nan	1982
Maureen	1984
Patricia Clare	1984
Helen Julian	1988
Judith Ann	1990
Chris	1992
Christine James	1992
Beverley	1998
Sue	1999
Frances (Society of the Holy Cross)	2001
Life Profession CSF 2009	
Jemma (Society of the Holy Cross)	2001
Life Profession CSF 2009	
Liz	2007

Province of the Americas

Cecilia	1967
Jean	1970
Ruth	1973
Pamela Clare	1981
Maggie	2007

Departed	**Date**

European Province

Margaret Mary	1946
Helen Elizabeth	1950
Mary Grace	1954
Mary Clare	1963
Lilian Agnes	1968
Muriel	1971
Anne	1977
Mildred	1982
Agnes Mary	1983
Bridget Fiona	1983
Mary Francis	1993
Leonore	1997
Angela Mary	1998
Barbara	1998
Gabriel	1999
Veronica	2001
Alison Mary	2003
Jennie	2008
Jenny Tee	2013
Teresa	2013
Angela Helen	2015

Province of the Americas

Elizabeth Ann	2001

Appendix 2

Principles of the First Order

Historical Note

The Principles are in large measure derived from the documents of the Christa Seva Sangha, a Brotherhood established in 1922 in Poona, India.

They were revised in 1930 for the Brotherhood of the Love of Christ, St Ives, Huntingdonshire, and again in 1937 when the Brotherhood of Saint Francis of Assisi, Hilfield, Dorset, amalgamated with them to form the Society of Saint Francis.

In 1967, the Order of Saint Francis, at Mount Sinai, New York, united with the Society of Saint Francis and *The Principles* were adopted as part of the Rule of the Brothers of the First Order. The Community of Saint Francis, a Sisterhood founded in 1905 in England, became a part of the Society of Saint Francis in 1964 and adopted *The Principles* as part of its Rule. In 1973, they were recognized as the Sisters of the First Order.

The text used is that generally in use prior to 1966, but now with inclusive language and biblical quotations from The New Revised Standard Version of the Bible.

The Principles are arranged for daily reading over the month.

Authorization

This text of *The Principles* was authorized as part of the Rule of the First Order of the Society of Saint Francis by a Joint Meeting of the Chapters of the Brothers and Sisters of the First Order in 1993, and ratified by the Joint Meeting of the Chapters in 1996.

Copyright © The Society of Saint Francis

Appendix 3

The Object of the Order

Day 1

Jesus the Master speaks, *Very truly, I tell you, unless a grain of wheat falls into the earth and dies, it remains just a single grain; but if it dies, it bears much fruit. Those who love their life lose it, and those who hate their life in this world will keep it for eternal life. Whoever serves me must follow me, and where I am, there will my servant be also. Whoever serves me, the Father will honour.* (John 12.24–26)

The Master sets before us in the example of his own sacrifice the secret of fruit-bearing. He surrenders himself to death, and lo! he becomes the source of new life to myriads. Lifted up from the earth in sacrifice, he draws unto him all those multitudes of which the Greeks, whose coming kindled his

vision, are the foretaste and prophecy. The life that is cherished perishes: the life that is renounced is eternal. (cf. John 12.20–21)

Day 2

This law of renunciation and sacrifice, which is the law of the Master's own life and fruit-bearing, he lays also upon his servants, bidding them follow him in the same path. To those who thus follow he promises the ineffable reward of union with himself and acceptance by the Father.

The object, therefore, of the First Order, is to build up a body of men and women who, accepting Christ as their Lord and Master, will seek to follow him in the way of renunciation and sacrifice as an act of witness and for the loving service of his Brothers and Sisters in the world.

7

The Three Conditions of Life

Day 3

The community, recognising that God has at all times called certain of his children to embrace a state of celibacy for the kingdom of heaven's sake, that they may be free to give themselves without distraction to his service, sets before itself the aim of building up a body of men and women who shall be completely dedicated to him alone both in body and spirit. These, after a sufficient period of probation, voluntarily in response to God's call, dedicate themselves to a life of devotion to our Lord under the conditions of poverty, chastity and obedience.

Day 4

It is not without reason that these three conditions have ever been embraced by those desiring to live the life of religious detachment; for they stand for the ideal of perfect renunciation of the world, the flesh and the devil, which are the three great enemies of the spiritual life.

Poverty

Day 5

The Master willingly embraced a life of poverty in this world. *He was rich, yet for your sakes he became poor.* (2 Corinthians 8.9)

He chose a stable for his birthplace and for his upbringing the house of a village carpenter. Even that home he left in early manhood and became a wayfarer, with *nowhere to lay his head.* (Matthew 8.20)

Us also he calls to poverty.

Whoever serves me must follow me. (John 12.26)

None of you can become my disciple if you do not give up all your possessions. (Luke 14.33)

The Brothers and Sisters, therefore, seek to be poor in spirit. They desire to escape from the love of the world and the things that are in the world and rather, like their patron St Francis, to be in love with poverty. They covet only the unsearchable riches of Christ. They recognise, indeed, that while some of their members may be called to a literal following of St Francis in a life of actual penury and extreme simplicity, for most so high an ideal will not be possible.

Day 6

The Brothers and Sisters desire to possess nothing which cannot be shared by those around them and such things as will help to satisfy their needs.

They receive no pay and own no personal possessions. They live as a family having all things in common. They receive for their use the simple necessities of life. Yet what they receive they regard not as their own but rather as lent to them for a season.

Nor must they, while excluding the snare of the world from their individual lives, allow it to return in the corporate community, where it may work a wider and more fatal destruction. It would be small gain were they to surrender their personal possessions only to live in luxury through the abundance of the common stock. Therefore the community must turn away from excess. The buildings it erects and the style and manner of life which it permits must be the simplest that are consistent with good health and efficient work. If there is money beyond what such simple needs require, let it be spent in works of mercy and service, or else be used for the house of God, which it is right and seemly with proper moderation to adorn, or for the purchase of books which are necessary to the work of study.

Day 7

In all things let the Brothers and Sisters exhibit the simplicity of true Franciscans who, caring little for the world where they are but strangers and pilgrims, have their hearts set on that spiritual home *where their treasure is.* (Matthew 6.21)

Chastity

Day 8

The Brothers and Sisters are bound, like all Christians, to resist and by God's grace to conquer the temptations of the flesh and to live lives of purity and self-control. They must ever strive through faithful self-discipline and prayer to be chaste both in mind and body.

Furthermore, that they may *promote unhindered devotion to the Lord* (1 Corinthians 7.35), and give themselves wholly to his work, being wedded only to Christ, their true spouse, they embrace of their own will the vocation of celibacy.

They do this not because they believe that the unmarried state is in itself higher than the married, but because they believe that for them the unmarried state is that in which God wishes them to serve him. Therefore they look to him with confidence to give them the grace needed for this life which, if they should undertake it contrary to his will, would be to them a state of greater rather than less distraction than that of marriage.

Day 9

In thus accepting the state of chastity, the Brothers and Sisters must ever be on their guard against the temptation to self-centeredness, coldness or a lack of sympathy with the interests of others. Their espousal to Christ must not weaken or mar their human affections. Rather must their union with him enable them to love more richly with his love all with whom they are brought in contact.

Obedience

Day 10

The Master, who, coming into the world not to do his own will but the will of him that sent him, *became obedient to the point of death – even death on a cross* (Philippians 2.8), says to those who follow him, *Take my yoke upon you, and learn from me; for I am gentle and humble in heart, and you will find rest for your souls.* (Matthew 11.29)

The Brothers and Sisters desire, therefore, to surrender their wills to the will of God, in the spirit of perfect obedience, that being delivered from self-will and pride they may find true freedom and peace and be ready instruments which he can use for his purposes.

Day 11

Further, by voluntarily accepting the Rule as binding upon them, the Brothers and Sisters pledge themselves to abide by this Rule and to obey the decisions of the Chapter, by which the common mind of the community is expressed and interpreted.

It is the work of the Ministers to administer the Rule and to see that the decisions of the Chapter are observed. Their directions, therefore, unless they order something contrary to the Rule or in itself sinful, must be promptly and cheerfully carried out. In their absence obedience is due to their Assistants. Brothers or Sisters put in charge of a department of work are also to be obeyed in that department. But none may on any authority act contrary to the guiding of their own consciences. The Ministers are, like the other members, under obedience to the Rule and Chapter and are bound to exercise their authority, not in a spirit of partiality or pride or selfishness, but with equal consideration and love and with humble prayer for the divine wisdom.

Day 12

The obligation of particular obedience within the community is gladly accepted by the members, not as something different from the obedience which they owe to God, but rather as part of that obedience. They are confident that, if God has called them to a life under Rule, they will, in fulfilling the obligations of that life, be most truly obeying him and that whatever limitations or humiliations their obedience may involve will, if cheerfully accepted, be a means by which pride is vanquished and a more perfect consecration achieved.

When working away from the community, the Brothers and Sisters should put themselves under the discipline of the parish or society in which they are staying.

The Three Ways of Service

Day 13

The Brothers and Sisters seek to serve their Master by the life of devotion, by sacred study and by works. In the life of the community as a whole all these three ways must find full and balanced expression. It is not, indeed, to be expected that all will devote themselves equally to each of these three tasks. It is right that their several employments should vary according to the particular ability which God has given them, as that some should, with the approval of their Minister, give themselves in large measure to prayer and contemplation, others to the pursuit of learning and the writing of books and others mainly to the ministry of active service. Yet must room be found in the lives of all for at least some measure of each of these three employments.

Prayer

Day 14

Praise and prayer constitute the atmosphere in which the Brothers and Sisters must strive to live. They must endeavour to maintain a constant recollection of the presence of God and of the unseen world. An ever-deepening devotion to Christ is the hidden source of all their strength and joy. He is for them the One all-lovely and adorable, God incarnate, crucified and risen, whose love is the inspiration of service and the reward of sacrifice.

Day 15

That their union with this Lord and Master may be ever renewed and strengthened, the Brothers and Sisters unite in offering daily before God the memorial of his death and passion and feeding often upon his sacrificial life. The Holy Eucharist is the centre round which their life revolves. It is above all the heart of their prayer life.

The time of morning prayer is the preparation of mind and spirit for entrance within the sanctuary. The meditation which follows later is the opportunity for quiet tryst with him who through the sacrament, is present inwardly, and for feeding on him in the heart by faith with thanksgiving.

The services of intercession and thanksgiving are times when those who have been thus joined with him in communion and meditation may plead with God in sure reliance on his promise: *If you abide in me, and my words abide in you, ask for whatever you wish, and it will be done for you* (John 15.7), and also thank him for continuous experience of its fulfilment.

The evening office is the renewed offering of praise and prayer to the same Lord at the end of the day's work, and in its closing silence the hearts of all are together steeped afresh in the peace of that inward uncreated light which, as the shadows of life deepen, abides unchanged. Compline is the Master's blessing of protection and peace.

Day 16

The Brothers and Sisters must strive ever to remember how essential is the work of prayer to every department of their lives. Without the constant renewal of divine grace the spirit flags, the will is weakened, the conscience grows dull, the mind loses its freshness and even the bodily vigour is impaired. They must, therefore, always be on their guard against the constant temptation to let other work encroach upon the hours of prayer, remembering that if they seek in this way to increase the bulk of their activity it can only be at the cost of its true quality and value.

They must be regular and punctual in their attendance at corporate prayer. They must also bear in mind that it is of little value to be present at the common devotions in a formal or careless spirit. They must seek to make of each office an offering of true devotion from the heart. The reverent, ordered and earnest offering of the corporate worship is the very heart of the community's life

Day 17

So, too, the Brothers and Sisters must guard with jealous watchfulness the times of private prayer.

They must remember that corporate worship is not a substitute for the quiet communion of the individual soul with God, and they must strive to go forward to ever fuller enjoyment of such communion, till they are living in so constant a remembrance of God's presence that they do indeed *pray without ceasing.* (1 Thessalonians 5.17)

Day 18

It is to assist such an attitude and practice of recollection that the rules of silence have been laid down and the Brothers and Sisters will welcome and use such silence, regarding it not as the imposition of an artificial restraint, nor merely as an external rule to be observed by refraining from speech, but as the opportunity for growing in the sense of the divine presence. They will welcome in a like spirit the retreats and days of quiet which the community's Rule provides as times when, in the withdrawal from all external distractions, the life of the spirit may be renewed and deepened.

In these and suchlike ways, the Brothers and Sisters will seek to keep ever fresh and living their devotion to Christ their Lord; and when through human frailty they fail in their high endeavour, they will yet return again to Christ with humble contrition and earnest purpose of amendment; and they will hold in special esteem that sacrament of penance and absolution whereby they are cleansed from sin and renewed in the life of grace.

Study

Day 19

The true knowledge is the knowledge of God. The highest wisdom is that holy wisdom whereby the soul is made one with God. The first place, therefore, in the Brothers' and Sisters' work of study will always be given to the study and practice of the way of the soul's ascent to God and the devotional study of the scriptures as one of the chief aids to that end. They will study also the teaching of the Christian saints concerning the spiritual life.

It is the hope of the community that some of its houses may be not only homes of prayer but also homes of learning. It is out of this recognition of the value and importance of study that some of the hours each day are set apart for this purpose under the Rule; and it is mainly for the uninterrupted securing of these hours that the rule of the lesser silence is laid down whenever possible.

Works

Day 20

Jesus the Master took on himself the form of a servant. *He came not to be served but to serve.* (Mark 10.45)

He went about doing good; curing all who were sick; bringing good news to the poor; binding up the broken-hearted. (Acts 10.38), (Matthew 8.16) Those who would claim to be his servants and follow him must be diligent in ministry to others. (Luke 4.18), (Isaiah 61.1)

The active works by which the Brothers and Sisters seek to serve their Master begin within the house and garden. (1 Thessalonians 5.17)

The sweeping, dusting and other menial offices, as well as certain forms of manual work, are apportioned among them so that all may contribute their share to the work of the household and the cost of their own living. All must be capable of engaging in some form of manual work. All must consider the interests of the community in its work for God and study strict economy. Brothers and Sisters will do their own work as far as possible. St Francis said that *the idle (member) has no place in the community.*

Day 21

Outside the special works of service to the community itself there are many opportunities of ministry, particularly to the uncared-for, the sick, the suffering and needy. The community sets before it, as the special programme of service which it would like to be able to carry out, those acts of mercy the doing of which even to the humblest the Master declares that he will accept as done unto himself. By helping in the relief of poverty we may give him food and drink. By hospitality to strangers we may take him in. By relieving those homeless and naked we may clothe him. By caring for the sick we may relieve him. By visiting the prisoners we may cheer him (cf. Matthew 25.35–45).

The community does not, indeed, expect ever to have at its disposal many funds for the administration of charitable relief, but it will gladly lend its members in the work of such relief and co-operate with others who are doing it. In all such work, the community will seek to serve all irrespective of creed, offering its services not as a bribe but as a reflection of the love of Christ himself.

Day 22

But chiefest of all forms of service that the Brothers and Sisters can offer must ever be the effort to show others in his beauty and power the Christ who is the inspiration and joy of their own lives. They will seek to do this, not in a spirit of aggression, nor with contempt for the beliefs of others, but rather because, knowing in their own experience the power of Christ to save from sin and to give newness of life, they must needs seek to share their own supreme treasure. Out of the fullness, therefore, of devoted love they would seek to give their belovèd Master to all.

They must remember that, in this task of showing Christ to others the witness of life is more eloquent than that of words. Franciscans must, therefore, seek rather to be living lives through which Christ can manifest himself than to preach much in public. Nevertheless, there will be some among them called more particularly to the ministry of the Word, and all must be ready at all times to give an answer for the faith that is in them (cf. 1 Peter 3.15), and particularly to guide all who are sincerely seeking after truth. They must also be ready by instruction and prayer and spiritual direction to strengthen the faith of Christians and lead them forward in the spiritual life.

Day 23

The Brothers and Sisters must be glad at all times to relieve those who come to them for help or counsel. They must never give the impression that they have no time for such ministry. Rather must they be ready to lay aside all other work, including even the work of prayer, where such service is immediately required, confident that such a negligence will surely be well-pleasing to the Servant of all.

The Three Notes of the Order

Day 24

The three notes which must ever in special degree mark the lives of the Brothers and Sisters are humility, love and joy. If these prevail within its members, the object of the community will be fulfilled and its work fruitful. If they are lacking, it will be unprofitable and barren.

Humility

Day 25

The Brothers and Sisters will strive to keep ever before them the example of him who *emptied himself, taking the form of a slave* (Philippians 2.7), and who, on the last night of his life, humbly in the guise of a slave washed his disciples' feet (cf. John 13.4–5). They will ever seek after his pattern to *clothe themselves with humility in their dealings with one another.* (1 Peter 5.5) Humility is the recognition of the truth about God and ourselves, the recognition of our own insufficiency and dependence, seeing that we have nothing which we have not received. It is the mother of all Christian virtues. As St Bernard of Clairvaux has said, *No spiritual house can stand for a moment save on the foundation of humility.* It is the first condition of a happy life within the family.

Thus those in the house must remember that Brothers and Sisters who are always confident that they are right and eager to impose their opinion on others, will themselves be unhappy as chafing under the discipline of subordination and correction and will also make the life of the family unhappy by marring that distinctive atmosphere of harmony and order which depends on everyone doing their allotted task with cheerfulness. The glad acceptance of the rule of obedience, and the loyal fulfilment of orders that are distasteful or difficult, will be one sure means of growing in this grace.

Day 26

The Brothers and Sisters must also refrain from all contemptuous thoughts one of another, and not seeking for pre-eminence must *regard others as better than themselves.* (Philippians 2.3)

The faults that they see in others must be subjects for prayer rather than criticism and they must be more diligent to *take the log out of their own eye* than *the speck out of their neighbour's eye.* (Matthew 7.5)

They must be ready not only gladly, *when invited, to go and sit down at the lowest place* (Luke 14.10), but rather of their own accord take it. Nevertheless, if entrusted with a work of which they feel incapable or unworthy, they must not shrink from accepting it on the plea of humility, but attempt it confidently through *the power (of Christ) made perfect in weakness.* (2 Corinthians 12.9)

In their relations also with those outside, the Brothers and Sisters must strive to show their Master's humility. They must welcome gladly all opportunities of humble service that come to them and never desire pre-eminence or praise. In particular they must resist the temptation to consider themselves superior to others because dedicated to a life of religion, realising how much greater often are the sacrifices and difficulties of those engaged in the ordinary professions of life and how much more nobly they face them.

Love

Day 27

The Master says, *By this everyone will know that you are my disciples, if you have love for one another.* (John 13.35)

Love is thus the distinguishing feature of all true disciples of Christ. It must be specially an outstanding note in the lives of those who are seeking to be specially consecrated to Christ as his servants. *God is love* (1 John 4.8) and, for those whose lives are *hidden with Christ in God* (Colossians 3.3), love will be the very atmosphere which surrounds all that they do.

This love the Brothers and Sisters must show towards all to whom they are united by natural ties of relationship or friendship. They will love them not less but more as their love for Christ grows deeper.

They will love also with a special affection those to whom they are united within the family of the community, praying for each individually and seeking to grow in love for each. They must be on their guard against all that injures this love: the bitter thought, the hasty retort, the angry gesture; and never fail to ask forgiveness of any against whom they have sinned. They must seek to love equally with others those with whom they have least natural affinity. For this love of one another is not simply the welling up of natural affection but a supernatural love which God gives them through their common union with Christ. As such it bears testimony to its divine origin. Our Lord intended the unity of those who believe in him to be a special witness to the world of his divine mission. The community must show the spectacle of a Christian family whose members, even though they be of varied race and education and character, are bound into a living fellowship by this supernatural love.

Lastly, in all their relationships with those, whether Christians or not, with whom their work brings them in contact they will seek to show forth this same supernatural Christ-like love; and, remembering that love is measured by sacrifice, they will seek gladly to spend whatever gifts they may possess of body, mind and spirit in the service of those to whom God calls them to minister.

Joy

Day 28

Finally, the Brothers and Sisters, *rejoicing in the Lord always* (Philippians 4.4), must show forth in their lives the grace and beauty of divine joy. They must remember that they follow the Son of Man, who came *eating and drinking* (Luke 7.34), who loved the birds and the flowers, who blessed little children (cf Mark 10.16), who was *a friend of tax collectors and sinners* (Matthew 11.19), who sat at the tables alike of the rich and the poor. They will, therefore, put aside all gloom and moroseness, all undue aloofness from the common interests of people and delight in laughter and good fellowship. They will rejoice in God's world and all its beauty and its living creatures, *calling (nothing) profane or unclean.* (Acts 10.28)

They will mingle freely with all kinds of people, seeking to banish sorrow and to bring good cheer into other lives. They will carry with them an inner secret of happiness and peace which all will feel, if they may not know its source.

Day 29

This joy, likewise, is a divine gift and comes only from union with God in Christ. As such it can abide even in days of darkness and difficulty, giving cheerful courage in the face of disappointment and an inward serenity and confidence in sickness and suffering. Those who possess it can be *content with weaknesses, insults, hardships, persecutions, and calamities for the sake of Christ; for whenever they are weak, then they are strong.* (2 Corinthians 12.10)

Day 30

These three notes of humility, love and joy, which should mark the lives of the Brothers and Sisters, are all supernatural graces which can be won only from the divine bounty. They can never be attained through our own unaided exertions. They are miraculous gifts of the Holy Spirit. But it is the purpose of Christ our Master to work miracles through his servants; and, if they will but be emptied of self and utterly surrendered to him, they will become chosen vessels of his Spirit and effective instruments of his mighty working, *who is able to accomplish abundantly far more than all we can ask or imagine.* (Ephisians 3.20).

Index of Names and Subjects

Index of Names and Subjects

Index of Bible References

Isaiah

53.5	2
61.1	62, 181

Matthew

5.10	30
6.21	175
7.5	141, 184
8.16	62, 181
8.20	45, 50, 174
11.19	132, 186
11.29	22, 176
16.24	13
19.29–30	13
25.31–46	49
25.35–45	79, 182
25.40	2, 17

Mark

10.16	132, 186
10.45	62, 181

Luke

4.18	62, 181
7.34	132, 186
9.58	50
14.10	141, 184
14.33	45, 174

John

12.2021	1, 173
12.24–26	1, 173
12.26	45, 174
13.35	ix, 185
13.4–5	183
15.7	153, 179

Acts

10.28	132, 186
10.38	62, 181

1 Corinthians

1.21	51
7.35	176

2 Corinthians

8.9	45, 174
12.9	141, 184
12.10	186

Ephisians

3.20	187

Philippians

1.11	50
2.3	141, 184
2.5–8	158
2.6–8	50
2.7	183
2.8	22, 176
4.4	132, 186

Colossians

3.3	ix, 185

1 Thessalonians

5.17	180, 181

1 Peter

2.9	159
3.15	101, 182
5.5	183

1 John

4.8	ix, 185